SHAPES
OF
CULTURE

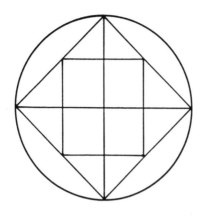

SHAPES OF CULTURE

THOMAS McFARLAND

UNIVERSITY OF IOWA PRESS

IOWA CITY

University of Iowa Press, Iowa City 52242
Copyright © 1987 by the University of Iowa
All rights reserved
Printed in the United States of America
First edition, 1987

Book and jacket design by Richard Hendel
Typesetting by G & S Typesetters, Austin, Texas
Printing and binding by Edwards Brothers, Ann Arbor, Michigan

Library of Congress Cataloging-in-Publication Data

McFarland, Thomas, 1926–
  Shapes of culture.

  Includes index.
  I. Culture. I. Title.
HM101.M34 1987   306   86-14670
ISBN 0-87745-162-1

For

my dear friends

Albert and Carol Cook

CONTENTS

ACKNOWLEDGMENTS

The substance of this book was delivered as the Ida Beam Lectures at the University of Iowa. I wish to take this occasion to thank my friends in the Department of English and in the Program in Comparative Literature, especially John E. Grant and Mary Lynn Johnson, Rudolf and Cecile Kuenzli, and Donald Marshall, for their gracious hospitality that made my sojourn in Iowa City so memorable and so pleasurable.

No part of this volume has previously appeared in print.

FOREWORD

Heidegger makes a distinction between talk that is chatter (*Gerede*) and talk that is authentic discourse (*Rede*). Though the ensuing pages may often seem to partake of chatter, or at least of some aspects of chatter, in that they seem anecdotal, at times only half serious, and at other times quite willing to meander from great texts to trivial pursuits, their true nature is paradoxical: *Gerede* that seeks to constitute itself as *Rede*.

Why not, one asks, simply *reden* if *Rede* is my aim? The answer to that perplexity will, I hope, emerge in the nature of the statements I shall be making in my chatter. Perhaps it will not, however, for the answer is both complex and not readily apparent. One part of it is that this book represents a subversion of any conventionally formal view of culture such as might be honored by a scholarly alignment of thesis, research, documentation, and conclusion, with discourse in an appropriately academic tone.

Such culture aspires to be cumulative, interrelated, and in its structure teleological, proceeding in chronologically linear sequence to a postulated goal whose importance is acknowledged by the community of scholars. The goal, however, eludes attainment. "In 1929," notes O. B. Hardison in questioning the efficacy of the aspiration, "Norman Foerster complained of the scholarly 'mystique of the brick,' according to which each new literary monograph is a brick stored in a gigantic brickyard for use by an architect who never comes." In any event, and wherever the architect may be, the present volume, even without its chatter, could hardly qualify for inclusion in the scholar's brickyard. It has neither the outline that would allow it to be stacked with the other bricks nor the composition that results in the necessary size, color, and weight. Especially as to this last, the work has nothing whatever to do with a requisite mass of research and documentation.

What is it about, then? A cataloguer for a library might willy-nilly have to declare the volume to be a contribution to the theory of meaning, or possibly an essay in the theory of value; alternatively, it might be catalogued as a study in the theory of translation, or, again, as an exercise in hermeneutics. But though there might seem to be some surface justification for any one of those placements, in fact the book has only tangential relation to any form of culture. It is, on the contrary and in validation of its title, solely identifiable as a shape of culture. The fourth chapter deliberately—or, ironically put, formally—generates such a shape. The entire volume, moreover, constitutes and reflexively illustrates what it is talking about: the work is not a form of culture but rather a shape of culture.

What is its tendency, then? Many readers might have difficulty seeing the book's point. Not that its chapters will be obscure in their language; in their local textures they should be quite clear. But some will perhaps have difficulty in seeing what it is doing, and others may glimpse something of what it is doing and be resistant, unconvinced, possibly even outraged. Still others might be less resistant and less unconvinced, but then they might be sad and feel themselves in the precincts of nihilism.

To the two latter classes of readers, I might reply as did the boy who took the Rorschach inkblot tests to the psychologist who administered them: "But doctor, you're the one who owns the dirty pictures." I shall not be arguing that there is no meaning connected with human culture. Nor shall I argue that human experience itself is devoid of meaning. Possibly, however, it might seem that I shall be arguing that there is not very much meaning in human experience, and that what meaning there is is unpredictable and evanescent. I might seem to be arguing that the absence of meaning, rather than the presence of meaning, generates the concerns of culture; that the experience of meaning that motivates cultural endeavor has always been restricted to the few; that the rest of the enormous throng of cultural participants is borne along by sociological, not cultural, currents. I am reluctant to endorse any of these unpleasant propositions, however, so I tack before the winds, chatter, whirl around the periphery, and allow my readers either to spin out to calmer waters or to plunge down the vortex.

Callimachus said that a big book is a bad thing. In recent years I find that I as a reader am increasingly grateful when a volume reveals its secrets to me in a day or an evening, rather than resisting over a period of weeks. Although I myself have been guilty of writing big books in the past, this one is written with the aesthetic aim of escaping the interdiction of Callimachus. But the reasons for its brevity are not alone aesthetic; they are dictated as well by the design of its meaning. "Plato," notes Karl Jaspers, "created a written work that for depth and greatness has no equal in all the history of philosophy." "And yet," continues Jaspers, "in his own judgment this lifework consisted merely of intimations and reminiscences." Of intimation and reminiscence too is this book constituted. Rather than aspiring to exhaustive treatment of its topics, it seeks to suggest, to hint, to insinuate. It thereby hopes to engage its readers in its enterprise by summoning them to supply, out of their own culture, the continuations merely pointed toward here, and to augment the cultural illustrations given only in their rudiments.

With the aim of enlisting each reader as a kind of coauthor, therefore, the book presents its brevity as an invitation, just as the intent of its scholarly anarchy is to reflect the larger situation of the cultural reality of our time.

I
THE
DECLINE
OF
CULTURAL
FORMS

This volume is concerned with intellectual densities that it calls shapes of culture. To some extent it attempts to describe their nature, which is variable; to chart their surfaces, which are protean; and to probe their masses, which range from the huge to the minute. Because it will deal with matters for which no previous formulations exist, it will attempt to illustrate its contentions not only with publicly accessible examples but also with anecdotes, ephemera, private recollections, and personal testimony.

It must be emphasized that the densities dealt with here are not forms of culture but shapes of culture. Form suggests something definite and linear, Euclidean: a straight line, a rectangle, a polyhedron. Shape, on the other hand, suggests something more amorphous and less privileged. If the book examined poems or novels or plays, or even, like Kenneth Burke, a political constitution, it would be examining forms of culture. So too if it were examining the criticism of poetry, the history of the novel, the theory of the drama, or the science of politics.

The difference between shape and form, though not usually discriminated in daily speech, is everywhere to be encountered, even outside the arena of culture. An especially dramatic example is supplied by the motion picture 2001, in the classic sequence where the geometrically defined metallic monolith is discovered on the moon. The journey from the space station to the lunar excavation is a passage through shapes, those outlines that comprise everyone's awareness of the moon's landscape. Still passing through random shapes, the scientists emerge into the excavated and eerily lighted pit, where suddenly, in a moment of great dramatic power, they view the startling and portentous rectangular form, generated by design, placed with intent, related to purpose. It is this, the interlocking of design, intent, relationship, and purpose, as opposed to the heterogeneous outlines and masses encountered as the random shapes of the lunar landscape, that supplies the drama. Above all, the lack of understanding of what the relationship of the object to its design and purpose might be, along with the equal opaqueness of its origin, paradoxically emphasizes the centrality of relationship to its conception; for the object thunderously demands these completions.

Relationship, indeed, is the essential condition of the object's form, its geometric structure merely the symbol of that condition. The lunar shapes, on the other hand, exist outside such requirement; they simply are. By the same token, to take another example, the stone heads on Easter Island are forms; the rocks beside them, shapes. Again, to view a pearl just extracted from an oyster is to cognize a shape; to see a string of pearls around a throat is to cognize a form.

Cultural units may exist either as form or as shape. Shapes of culture, however, though everywhere to be encountered, are not customarily noted, or if noted, are not examined. They frequently, and at this day characteristically, masquerade under the prestige attached to forms of culture. Indeed, when shapes masquerade as forms, they exhibit no discernible difference with respect to inert structure. The difference, then, lies solely in the direction of the cultural energy of the two entities, which is circular and inward, centripetal, in the shapes; outward and linear, centrifugal, in the forms. Shapes of culture tend toward self-referentiality; forms, toward reticulation with other forms.

Otherwise the status of shapes of culture is not unlike what Santayana, in *Skepticism and Animal Faith,* calls "essences"; they are what they are. They have no relations among themselves except as elements in that general field of educated awareness that we call culture. Their geometry is more like that of unpredictably curved Riemannian surface than that of Euclidean line and angle.

Though they do not relate among themselves, shapes of culture constitute. When we see photographs of units such as molecules taken through an electron microscope, the units seem to be blobs in a common field; that is, they are shapes, not forms. The same holds true, a fortiori, for smaller particles. If we attend to a cinematic documentary about the origins of life, the closer to origins we come the more without form, but the more ineluctably as shape, do the protoplasmic entities of blob and slime reveal themselves. Shape is more primordial than form, and shape is what is left when form breaks down. A junkyard is full of shapes, though its forms are dismembered.

Shape as such is a multiplex unity, not a relation with other shapes. On a cultural plane, shape in its highest manifestation is a unitive mystery analogous to melody in musical composition. A melody is a unit, but it must be made of a plurality of notes, not of a single note. It can occur in a musical composition consisting of other notes, but it must occur unitively, and when it is used in different combinations in the same or other compositions, it must still be unitive. The variations of the "harmonious blacksmith" melody in Handel's Fifth Suite for Harpsichord in E Major unfold like the progressively more complex configurations of a bud opening into a flower, but throughout all the recombinations, the same unitive core is identifiable. The suite itself is a form; its melody is a shape.

Exactly what melody is in any other sense, no one has ever been able to say. All definitions are like a mathematical definition of the color red, which utterly cannot substitute for the actual seeing of red. No musicological formulation in any way penetrates the coincidence of the many and the one that constitutes melody; melody is not heard with the ear, for the ear hears only notes, and the melodic unity is recognized only by the kind of unitive intuition that we might refer to by the word *soul*. Such a concept is customarily invoked when we are in the presence of the greatest music. For instance, when Heinrich von Kleist's uncle attended the first performance of Mozart's *La Clemenza di Tito* in 1791, the uncle, Franz von Kleist, wrote then that Mozart's melodies "are so beautiful as to entice the angels down to earth"; and after a performance of *Don Giovanni* four days later, he referred to Mozart as an "artist who can take from the spheres their harmony and delight men's souls with their tones." One is tempted, indeed, to claim that melody is the direct presentation, not a participation or *methexis,* of those archetypes that Plato called *paradeigmata.*

Melody occurs in music, but it is its own reality. Melody is assuredly not necessary to music. Some composers, even great ones, have no gift for melody; others, Mozart supremely, are prodigally endowed. Melody is not essential to music; melody is essential in itself. It is hardly an accident that Proust symbolized the unattainable absolute by invoking melody, which he described as the Vinteuil phrase. Should actual examples be required, there is a melody in the last movement of Schumann's Second Symphony that will serve as well as any to point to the mystery, the unitive integrity, and the untranslatability of this ultimate shape. There is another in Schubert's Fifth Symphony—though neither symphony nor melody is his finest—that caused tears to well in my eyes the first time I heard it, a boy standing in a record-shop booth, in a distant city and an earlier time. In Mozart, the melodic ultimate can be heard again and again—in the first and last movements of the Twenty-first Quartet in D Major, for instance. In Mozart's Twenty-fifth Piano Concerto in C Major, just before the end of the last movement, the ultimate obtrudes so briefly and subtly that many pianists efface it by the wrong tempo or dynamics.

The ultimate, however, is the rarely attained boundary of what are here called shapes of culture; the illustrative material to be adduced for such shapes is for the most part not referred to such boundary but is rather prized out of the thick textures of cultural *écriture.* The illustrations, though brief, are urgent, because shapes of culture— whether we are aware of it or not, and most of us are at least subliminally aware, lacking only a nomenclature to bring the matter to conscious attention—have more and more become the substance of our knowledge.

Yet it was not always thus. Francis Bacon told Lord Burghley that he took "all knowledge" for his province, and in *The Advancement of Learning* and its Latin amplification he set out to survey all the interrelated forms of culture existent in his day. He was not claiming, however, to know all of reality, just all forms of culture. He had not, for instance, been to China and was not anticipating that he would go. He was saying, rather, that all forms of culture having to do even with knowledge of China either were within, or by extension could easily be brought within, his purview.

Bacon's ideal carried over into the thought of his most illustrious seventeenth-century successors. As Ernst Cassirer has pointed out, in his volume translated as *The Problem of Knowledge,* the idea of a universal knowledge was essential to the conception of culture:

> The thought of the *mathesis universalis* [universal knowledge] as it opened up before the mind of Descartes in his first great discovery, analytical geometry, is the common bond uniting every part of the Cartesian philosophy with every other part into one indissoluble whole. Even mathematics, so Descartes declared in his *Rules for the Direction of the Mind,* cannot fulfill its true philosophical mission as long as it is satisfied with only solutions of partial problems, and is nothing more than a theory of figures or numbers. So considered, it remains but an ingenious and sterile intellectual game. It will be really understood in principle and its philosophical import recognized only when it succeeds in advancing from a special to a universal science—a science of all that can be reduced to order and measure and thus is accurately known. . . .
>
> The same spirit also dominates the philosophy of Leibniz and inspires all its special doctrines. The plan of a universal encyclopedia is the. grand leading motive of all his scientific and philosophical inquiry. It attended him all life long, and there is no single work that does not relate to it in some way or another; everything focuses on this one central point. Hence there is no waste or dispersion in the immeasurable fullness of Leibniz's creativity.

But the advancement of learning, unforeseen by its seventeenth-century adherents, has in our own day become the fragmentation of learning as well. In the university, which has traditionally been the guardian of cultural forms, there is perhaps no chair of more prestige in mathematics than the Lucasian Professorship of Mathematics at Cambridge, now held by the eminent mathematical physicist Stephen Hawking. Likewise, there is perhaps no chair of classical learning with greater prestige than the Regius Professorship of Greek at that same university. One need hardly point out that in our own era the Regius Professor of Greek at Cambridge lives in an intellectual world unspeakably different from that of the Lucasian Professor of Mathematics; neither could possibly contribute to the sphere of the other, and it would seem ridiculously inappropriate to suggest that either should be expected to.

What do we say, however, to the fact that it was not always thus? The first holder of the Lucasian Professorship in Mathematics—the chair subsequently held by the mighty Newton—was Newton's teacher, Isaac Barrow; and our modern minds whirl when we realize that this same Isaac Barrow was also Regius Professor of Greek. Our minds become positively dizzy, furthermore, when we ponder the fact that Barrow, his attainments notwithstanding, was not so eminent, either in his command of mathematics or in his command of Greek, as was Leibniz; and our modern disorientation becomes complete when we realize that Leibniz in his own day was admired less as mathematician and classical scholar than as philosopher, historian, legal theorist, and diplomat. The population of the world has increased more than tenfold since Leibniz's time, and a greater proportion of that population is being educated today, but one can say with supreme confidence that there is not a single savant alive now who can even come within hailing distance of Leibniz's command of cultural forms. Even by the nineteenth century, such a claim as Bacon's to a purview of "all knowledge" could be made only in a context of irony, as in this quatrain about the Master of Balliol:

> Here stand I, my name is Jowett,
> If there's knowledge, then I know it;
> I am the master of this college,
> What I know not, is not knowledge

The derisory admiration from undergraduates was not only a testimonial to their own ignorance; it also covered deep unease at the real cultural situation. Not only was Jowett not particularly learned when compared to certain of his contemporaries in Germany and France, but even restricting the comparison to Oxford and to classi-

cal philology, he was hardly in the class of, say, Ingram Bywater—
not to speak of R. C. Jebb at Cambridge. Yet neither of these men,
their prowess in Greek notwithstanding, actually knew very much of
what there was to be known; and by their era the concerns of classical scholarship had become almost entirely a shape of culture. When
one of their number, the classical scholar A. W. Verrall, was in 1911
made the first holder of the King Edward VII Professorship in English Literature at Cambridge, his move to the new form of culture
had something of the character of an Eskimo leaping from a melting
ice floe to what at that time seemed like firm land.

It had not always been thus. The revival of classical learning that
signalized the Renaissance was fueled by the belief that command of
the ancient languages would uncover treasures of wisdom known by
antiquity and lost by the fifteenth century; Renaissance masters of
Greek and Latin such as Ficino, Poliziano, and Pico della Mirandola
approached Greek and Latin grammar with the expectation that it
would be a key to unlock great truths.

Gradually, however, the thinkers of Western Europe came to believe that perhaps they themselves could find those truths as well
or better than their ancient predecessors. Bacon suggested that the
thinkers of his time stood in relation to those of antiquity not as children who learned from wise parents but rather as adults who had
outgrown the concerns of childhood: "new discoveries must be
sought from the light of nature, not fetched back out of the darkness
of antiquity"; "men have been kept back as by a kind of enchant-
ment from progress in the sciences by reverence for antiquity";
"And to speak truly, *Antiquitas saeculi juventus mundi* [the antiquity
of time is the youth of the world]. These times are the ancient times,
when the world is ancient, and not those which we account ancient . . . by a computation backward from ourselves." In putting
forward these opinions, Bacon became the harbinger of a rapidly
changing situation. (Ben Jonson, for instance, praised several of his
immediate predecessors in Britain, among them and especially Bacon
himself, "who hath fill'd up all numbers; and perform'd that in our
tongue, which may be compar'd, or preferr'd, either to insolent
Greece, or haughty *Rome*.") Later on in the seventeenth century, the

querelle des anciens et des modernes unmistakably marked a watershed, in both France and England, between the reverence for antiquity and the new self-confidence of the modern world.

By the early nineteenth century, the study of the ancient languages, though strongly entrenched, was already beginning to veer from the temporal linearity of a form of culture to the self-referentiality of a shape of culture. Thus Hegel in 1809 perspicaciously defends the pertinence of the study of classical languages:

> For more than a thousand years Greece and Rome has been the soil on which all civilization has stood, from which it has sprung, and with which it has been in continuous connection. Just as the natural organisms, plants and animals, struggle to free themselves from gravitation without being able to renounce this element of their own nature, so the fine arts and the sciences have grown up on this soil, and, while they have attained a selfsubsistence of their own, they have not yet emancipated themselves from the recollection of that older culture. As Antaeus renewed his energies by touching his mother-earth, so every new impetus and invigoration of science and learning has emerged into the daylight from a return to antiquity.

Immediately following this homage, however, he begins to take note of a lessening relevance in the knowledge of Greek and Latin:

> But, however important the preservation of this soil is, the modification of the relation between antiquity and modern times is no less essential. . . . I need only remind you in a few words of the well-known position which the learning of the Latin language formerly had. It was regarded not simply as one element in education but was rather its most essential part and the only means of higher education offered to a pupil who refused to be satisfied with the general rudimentary education. . . . [But] a unanimous objection was raised against that learning of Latin, by now an obsolete language. In particular, it was felt that a nation cannot be considered civilized if it cannot express all the treasures of knowledge in its own language, if it

cannot move freely in that language whatever the topic discussed. . . . This new outlook, together with deficient methods that often degenerated into a merely mechanical procedure . . . has step by step destroyed the claim of Latin learning to be the citadel of all the sciences. This learning has lost the dignity so long claimed for it, the dignity of being the universal and almost the sole foundation of education.

Hegel goes on to praise the state for having set up a second, parallel, scientific and technical education "independently of the ancient literatures." Denying the implications of what he has just conceded, he claims that this development actually makes classical learning more secure:

The study of the ancient languages is preserved. . . . It has lost its exclusive character, because it now takes its place alongside those other modes of education and methods of attaining science, and in this way it may have extinguished the hatred aroused by its former arrogance. Thus as one separate discipline alongside others, it has all the more right to demand that it shall be given free scope and that henceforward it shall remain less troubled by alien and disturbing intrusions.

By this segregation and restriction it has obtained its true position and the opportunity of a freer and fuller development.

This is whistling past the graveyard indeed. For our present argument, however, we should see it less as "denial" than as reconceiving what had heretofore been a form of culture as a shape of culture. To that end, Hegel, having allowed so much of the claim to access to knowledge to be taken away from the classical languages, must resort to a different rhetoric to justify their continued study:

. . . if we agree that excellence should be our starting-point, then the foundation of higher study must be and remain Greek literature in the first place, Roman in the second. The perfection and glory of those masterpieces must be the spiritual bath, the secular baptism that first and indelibly attunes and tinctures the soul in respect of taste and knowledge.

Again: "I do not believe I claim too much when I say that he who has never known the works of the ancients has lived without knowing what beauty is." And yet again: "The works of the ancients contain the most noble food in the most noble form: golden apples in silver bowls."

He now must argue, the access to true knowledge no longer being posited as the goal of the study of ancient languages, that the very remoteness of the study is beneficial: ". . . the soul must always be provided with the means of estranging itself from its natural condition . . . the young mind must be led into a remote and foreign world." The study of grammar necessary to acquire the languages must likewise now be seen as a good in itself:

> . . . in learning grammar, therefore, the understanding itself first becomes learned . . . grammar expounds the categories of understanding in a fashion adapted to youth. . . . Grammatical terminology teaches us how to move in the realm of abstractions. This study consequently can be looked on as a preliminary instruction in philosophy. . . . Grammatical learning of an *ancient* language affords the advantage of necessarily implying a continuous and sustained activity of reason.

In brief, though still identifiable as a form of culture, by Hegel's time the study of Greek and Latin was already being diverted into future encapsulation as a shape of culture.

The seeds of the dissolution of classical studies as a form of culture are in Hegel's defense already clearly visible as sproutings. A century later, when Verrall ascended to the King Edward VII Chair in English Literature at Cambridge, the sproutings had become a luxuriant growth. Verrall, in moving from classical studies to English studies, was moving from a discipline that had been transmuted into a shape of culture to one that was becoming a new form of culture.

To be sure, the knowledge of Greek and Latin at Cambridge had hardly ever reached greater refinement than it did at this time. But that is precisely the point: its expertness was channeled into self-referentiality as a shape of culture, not into continuing pertinence as a form of culture. The only real use of Greek, indeed, was as a kind of passport to social heights, much as being born into a ducal family was. In 1906, for instance, George Bernard Shaw had a character in his *Major Barbara* (the character was modeled on Gilbert Murray, who was to become Regius Professor of Greek at Oxford) speak as follows: "Let me advise you to study Greek, Mr. Undershaft. Greek scholars are privileged men. Few of them know Greek; and none of them know anything else; but their position is unchallengeable. Other languages are the qualifications of waiters and commercial travellers: Greek is to a man of position what the hallmark is to silver." The almost blossomlike perfection of classical studies in the first decade of the twentieth century in England was a self-enclosed expansion of the special conditions of that epoch, not a form of culture.

Nothing else, indeed, can account for the nugatory status of Verrall's later reputation. He was not a trivial man; on the contrary, the memorial volume of his essays, *Collected Literary Essays: Ancient and Modern*, published in 1913 with reminiscences and personal testimonials from his friends and students, reveals him, even under the pardonable hyperbole of the occasion, to have been a human being of extraordinary quality. Nor was he unproductive. In addition to the memorial essays he published no fewer than a dozen volumes in his career. Nor were his writings foolish. His prose style was elegant and incisive; he commanded the literatures of France and Italy as well as those of Greece, Rome, and England; his critical comment was sensitive and informed.

So why is he so wholly (except for a languid eddying in classical waters in our own day) without later effect? The answer seems clear: he functioned in a self-referential shape of culture. That shape was irregularly bounded by a classical expertise no longer relevant, by interpretations of authors—notably Euripides—who no longer needed them, and by a special audience cast up by the socioeconomic privilege of the Edwardian Establishment. Verrall's placement on the Cambridge faculty, at its inner vantage point of Trinity College, was as much a part of his cultural shape as was his preoccupation with Greek iambs and Latin prose style. Even the heartfelt tributes of his friends and admirers presuppose the niceties of a favored elite, and they refer to ways of living not possible to millions, either in his day or our own.

The earlier form of culture had now almost wholly changed into a shape, and it no longer had connection to the chronological linearities of form. Ficino, Poliziano, and Pico had looked into the past in order to proceed with more knowledge into the future, but Verrall seems to have suspected that his classical commitments were now eddying in a pool without outlet. ("Signs, however, indicate," he says in one of his essays, "that the long tutelage of mankind by Latin may soon end or be interrupted. Should this take place, one result may be that those who do go to Latin will go to it more for pleasure and less for literary training; and in that case, though Virgil and Horace will not descend, the reputation of Propertius will relatively rise, as in fact it has lately risen.") And he made the leap from his Edwardian classicist's ice floe to the new form of English literature too late, for he died soon after assuming the chair.

The new form, English studies, seemed for a while to focus the richest possibilities of culture. Its most influential annunciator, F. R. Leavis, dominating the Cambridge scene a quarter of a century after Verrall's demise, exerted an influence undreamed of by his predecessor. Abjuring the special training and elitist conditions necessary for progress in the classical languages, Leavis made the very accessibility of English the foundation of his extraordinary effect. The native language of a country, he argued, provided the key to the values of its society, and the study of the great tradition of English literature was, for those born to the language and heritage of Britain, a key to spiritual enrichment, moral understanding, and practical intelligence far surpassing those attainable through the desiccated refractions of classical languages or of philosophy, even though "I shall not, I hope, be supposed to be banishing Classics and Philosophy from my ideal university. I am merely insisting that there is an essential discipline that must be found elsewhere."

That essential discipline and its elsewhere were the literature of England, and all Leavis's theoretical and practical efforts were devoted "towards making a School of English a real humane focus in a university, pre-eminently representative of the Idea, and capable of discharging the function of the university in the matter of liberal education." English was to be the core of the university, the "living principle" (one of Leavis's volumes was entitled *The Living Principle: 'English' as a Discipline of Thought*); and in its turn the university was to be the "humane centre" of civilization as such: "How to produce the 'educated man'—the man of humane culture who is equipped to be intelligent and responsible about the problems of contemporary civilization—this is a truly urgent study, but a study that apart from an adequate preoccupation with the Idea of a University is likely to end in despair."

But Leavis's high hopes for English studies as the center of the university and the university as the center of civilization, which were expressed with so much effect in the middle decades of this century, have foundered. Far from maintaining themselves as "a discipline of thought," English studies have become a grab bag of unrelated attitudes; from a form of culture they in their turn have metamorphosed into heterogeneous shapes of culture.

The reasons are intriguing. Classical studies were channeled from forms of culture into shapes of culture by their elitism and redundancy; English studies, on the other hand, were not elite at all, but rather proliferated so riotously that the larger outlines of their relevance broke down. Not elitism and redundancy, but popularity and facticity were the agents at work in their own transformation. Every book and article written on, say, Wordsworth, makes Wordsworth more difficult to command on a specialist level; and books and articles pour remorselessly from the press. In a single recent year, 1977, there were 2,184 books and articles published on Shakespeare alone (in 1979 the number was 2,859). To a lesser extent, the same kind of deluging publication drowns every canonical figure in English literature, with a consequent dampening of the possibilities of significant specialization. A corollary problem is that specialists increasingly cannot even very effectively extend their range to figures usually grouped with their nominal subject of study. For instance, eminent Wordsworthian scholars no longer tend to be reliable in their judgments and comments about Coleridge, who himself has elicited

flooding attention in recent years. The same effect holds from Coleridge back to Wordsworth, as it does between scholars specializing
in, say, Hardy on the one hand and Joyce on the other.

In the several decades since Leavis's influence reached its peak,
indeed, English studies have become almost totally fragmented into
disconnected and increasingly arbitrary shapes. Half a century ago,
for instance, a doctoral oral examination in English could still range,
even if only nominally, over the entirety of English literature. Doubtless it was always a fiction that anyone really knew the full range,
but at least it was a maintainable fiction. Now students customarily
understand that they need be responsible only for ever-contracting
segments cut out at random from that literature.

To be sure, there are attempts, spasmodic, sporadic, unsuccessful,
to break out of the centripetal force fields of shapes into a renewed
reticulation of forms. An article in the *New York Times* for 25 April
1986 tells, with glowing hope, of some of these attempts. Under a
headline, "Scholarly Disciplines: Breaking Out," it is reported that
"a dozen professors at Bryn Mawr College got together and formed
a private study group of a kind that has been popping up on cam-
puses around the country." The article continues:

> The professors had discovered that they were all feeling frus-
> trated by the narrowness of their separate departments, which
> included literature, philosophy, anthropology and art history.
>
> They wanted to ask bigger questions than their specialties
> usually encouraged them to ask. They wanted to know how
> other disciplines interpret the human world of language, knowl-
> edge and culture. . . .
>
> Out of such yearnings has come a current of change that is
> affecting the way academics think, write and teach. Some be-
> lieve it is challenging the basic structure of American univer-
> sities. "Groups and committees are being formed all over the
> country to break down the departmental system," said Steven
> Levine, an art historian who is a leader of the Bryn Mawr
> group, the Committee on Interpretation.

The piece goes on, with the kind of just-around-the-corner optimism
that characterizes articles on the impending control of schizophrenia

or the imminent cure of cancer (such articles are a genre, really), to talk of other professors—most of them in English departments—at other universities; and it concludes with happy if jejune high-mindedness:

> No one knows where the new interests will lead, but those most deeply involved tend to think that further specialization in the humanities and social sciences cannot continue indefinitely.
>
> "Students may eventually major in reading or writing rather [than] in things called history of art or anthropology or French," Professor Levine said. He said he hoped that cross-disciplinary efforts would make students and professors less narrow and "technocratic" and added, "I think it would make better citizens."
>
> Professor Cohen, of the University of Virginia, said that in his view the underlying message of the new study groups and their progeny was simple: "It indicates that education needs to be broadened, and that it can be broadened by people trying to relate what they do to what other people do."

Alas, it is later than the professors think. Recently a friend of mine in England enclosed two clippings in a single letter. One was an article in the *London Times* for 15 November 1985 commenting with dismay on the fact that the two most recent holders of the King Edward VII Chair in English Literature at Cambridge, Frank Kermode and Christopher Ricks, had in rapid succession resigned. The article is replete with gloom: "Cambridge English has had a new lease of apathy. In 1981, Frank Kermode resigned the King Edward VII professorship. . . . Several inspiring senior people have left since then." "There is a crisis of confidence in the subject too." "Bitterness may be in the Cambridge air, but the atmosphere became more fetid than ever when people began to disagree not over what literature means, but over whether there is literature." "Meanwhile, students are arriving less and less prepared for Cambridge life, socially and academically. They are widely considered less independent-minded and more fashion-conscious than before." The article concludes with foreboding: "Ricks has recently announced his resignation from the end of this academic year, after the shortest-ever tenure of the senior chair. There have been only five Edward VII professors since the chair was instituted in 1912; for two to resign within four years reinforces the feeling that there is something amiss."

Something is also amiss in English studies according to the second article, a review of a collection of American essays, published in 1985, called *Criticism in the University.* The review, written by Graham Hough and published in the *Observer,* begins: "The state of chronic hypochondria in which literary education subsists shows no sign of abating. Indeed, in some quarters it is entering an acute phase. Regular and formerly healthful activities lose their zest, attacked by morbid depression of spirits." After further comment in that vein, Hough continues:

> It is painfully evident among the contributors to *Criticism in the University* that practically everyone is bored and irritated by the teaching of literature on traditional lines, and more than doubtful whether it is doing any good to anyone. Besides irrelevant but heartfelt grouses about their salaries, conditions of tenure and prospects of promotion, some of these writers seem to feel a resentment amounting almost to hatred of their calling. Much of this no doubt lies deep in the sociology of academic life in general, but one can guess at more particular reasons. Not long ago Sir Peter Medawar remarked that when the momentous DNA discoveries were being made there were plenty of people in the English faculties of universities quite as clever as Crick and Watson—but Crick and Watson had something to be clever about. For the last thirty years or so ambitious literary exegetes have lacked precisely this—something to be clever about. Commentary and interpretation of the classic canon is by now so copious, so complete, that no addition to it is likely to matter very much. Most of the editing of any importance has been done. No creative upheaval like the Modernist movement of the earlier part of this century has come about, to make us redraw the map of literary history. So one has had the sad spectacle of many trim and high-powered intellectual machines with their wheels spinning in the air.

Hough goes on to note that the situation is being rectified by simply inventing problems to work on, and after examples directed to the French influence in modern criticism, concludes sardonically: "Now there was plenty to be clever about."

The fragmentation, arbitrariness, and virtually game-playing self-encapsulation of contemporary English studies are reflected in other putative forms of culture as well. The psychologist Jerome Bruner's autobiographical reminiscences, *In Search of Mind,* which for our purposes are especially interesting for his observations as a long-term faculty member at both Harvard and Oxford, are rich with data germane to the rise of shapes of culture. For instance, he notes that the study of psychology at Harvard broke off from the study of philosophy, with an accompanying increase in self-referentiality:

> As I reflect back on the "battle" to establish a cognitive emphasis in psychology, I am struck by an irony. The disciplined procedures for reflecting on one's own thoughts . . . are principally to be found outside psychology, principally in philosophy. My psychological "parents" at Harvard were all veterans of the battle to lead psychology out of the Philosophy Department. . . . But after all the struggles, I am finally convinced that a psychology of mind can never be free of a philosophy of mind.

But then psychology itself, as a new entity, again split into alternate shapes, with a consequent loss of relevance to formal goals:

> In 1946 the old Department of Psychology split. One wing . . . joined sociology and social anthropology, to found a new Department of Social Relations, an extraordinary collection: Talcott Parsons, Samuel Stouffer, Pitirim Sorokin, Gordon Allport, Henry Murray, Clyde Kluckhohn. . . . Social Relations eventually became focused upon larger, macrosociological issues. Psychology, perhaps in reaction, narrowed its focus to the details of operant conditioning and psychophysics. The heart of psychology—the study of the powers of mind and their enablement—fell neglected between the two.

The proliferation of commentary that swells knowledge until it bulges out of its original form and bursts into a cascade of specialist shapes, this is the distinctive phenomenon of the modern intellectual situation. Not only do specialists within the enclave of English literature peer toward the situation in, say, history like medieval barons peering from their castle walls toward a neighboring fortification, but they find unrest and alienation within their own domains. The enclaves themselves have broken up into groups and subgroups. Specialists in Renaissance literature at faculty meetings loll in open inattention when appointments in Victorian studies are being considered. Specialists in American literature cannot talk to medievalists— and both are unapologetic; specialists in sixteenth-century literature do not converse with specialists in eighteenth-century literature.

The situation, it must be emphasized, is not confined to English studies. Bruner's observations about the fragmentation of psychological studies find parallels in other cultural areas. I am reliably told, for instance, that at the present time specialists in one branch of mathematics have nothing to say to specialists in another branch. (No one—it is a further index to our endemic cultural fragmentation—would expect me to know that truth for myself.) Frege, who devoted himself to the foundations of mathematics, had only selective relationship to other mathematicians of his time; indeed, as reported in Michael Dummett's *Frege: Philosophy of Language,* the situation in the first quarter of this century provides choice views of the in-between or transitional state from interrelated forms of culture to self-enclosed shapes of culture:

> Among mathematicians, Frege had the respect of Dedekind and of Zermelo. Cantor, however, was hostile. In *Grundlagen* Frege made complimentary references to Cantor, which Cantor repaid by writing a savage and quite uncomprehending review of the book. . . . Frege wrote a brief reply, and retaliated by scoring points off Cantor in Volume II of *Grundgesetze.* Hilbert paid occasional tributes to Frege, for instance in his lecture in 1904 "Über die Grundlagen der Logik und der Arithmetik" to the International Congress of Mathematicians at Heidelberg; but he was content to dismiss his work as vitiated by the para-

doxes. Brouwer appears to have been totally unaware of Frege's existence, although Frege, as an arch-platonist, would have been the perfect object of his attack on classical mathematics, and indeed, some of his polemics would have been much more appropriately directed against Frege than against Hilbert. Peano had some correspondence with Frege, but foolishly did not take him very seriously or make much attempt to understand him. . . . With the exceptions I have mentioned, mathematicians and philosophers alike ignored him.

But though "in 1925 Frege died an embittered man, convinced both that he had been unjustly neglected, and that his life's work had been for the most part failure," he himself was no more attentive to the lifelines of cultural forms than those who ignored him:

Perhaps more remarkable than the continuity of his views is the total obliviousness which he displays to the work of others. By 1918, the subject of mathematical logic, invented by Frege, had received many profound contributions, from Russell and Whitehead, Hilbert, Zermelo, Löwenheim and others. It is true that, apart from Löwenheim's, these contributions related more to the foundations of mathematics than to elementary logic, about which Frege was concerned in these articles: but, although Frege had an extensive correspondence with Löwenheim, now unfortunately lost, there is not a trace in his published or unpublished writing of any notice on his part of the work that was going on in the field he had opened up; he writes, in the *Logische Untersuchungen,* as if no one had ever thought about these subjects before. . . . [H]is ideas in philosophy and mathematics are amazingly independent of stimulation from those of others.

That whole situation might profitably be contrasted to the intense interchanges and mutual awarenesses of seventeenth-century mathematics, with Leibniz studying the unpublished papers of Pascal, working on problems Bernoulli sent to him and Newton, adding the schematism of abscissa and ordinate to the analytic geometry of Descartes, being aware enough of the unpublished work of Newton that he was later caught up in a controversy about possible plagiarism in their twin conceptions of the differential calculus.

The modern situation in philosophy is hardly different from that just noted for Frege's mathematical and logical functioning. Not only has philosophy in this century largely divided along a watershed formed by positivist/analytic conceptions on the one hand and phenomenological/existentialist conceptions on the other, but by and large the adherents of the two modes have known little about one another and indeed have contemptuously dismissed the relevance or necessity of such knowledge. And the positivist/analytic group, at least, has customarily paid little attention to the historical linearity of past knowledge. For instance, in his review of Nelson Goodman's *The Structure of Appearances,* Dummett notes (the review is reprinted in his *Truth and Other Enigmas*), "No philosopher before 1900 is once mentioned: the only writers who are cited more than twice are Carnap, C. I. Lewis and Quine."

The fragmentation in historical reference is matched by fragmentation and encapsulation in topical reference. As Dummett says in an essay on Wittgenstein's philosophy of mathematics in the same volume: "I think that there is no ground for Wittgenstein's segregation of philosophy from mathematics but that this springs only from a general tendency of his to regard discourse as split up into a number of distinct islands with no communication between them (statements of natural science, of philosophy, of mathematics, of religion)."

On the other hand, to remain with *Truth and Other Enigmas* as source for examples, when Dummett angrily rejects the attack on Oxford Philosophy contained in Ernest Gellner's *Words and Things,* his line of defense is precisely to plead that such philosophy does not constitute a form but is rather a congeries of shapes: "Ernest Gellner's now celebrated little book is an attack on a philosophical school centred in Oxford, called 'linguistic philosophy'; in assessing it we have therefore to ask, 'Is there such a school?'" Dummett then points out that though "there was before the war an identifiable and self-conscious group of *révoltés* among the professional philosophers at Oxford," once victory was attained, "its cohesion fell away; . . . philosophers at Oxford ceased to think of themselves as belonging to any definite group or party."

Gellner, urges Dummett, not only sees cohesive forms where there are none, but he tries to lump together early and late work by the same philosopher; whereas, seems the thrust of Dummett's argument, such temporally discrete phases belong to different cultural shapes:

> As a serious piece of philosophical criticism, Gellner's book is wholly vitiated by his failure to distinguish between the different targets of his attack. He does indeed acknowledge that "linguistic philosophy" is not logical positivism; but in fact he attributes to it ideas that were in vogue only during the early stages of the revolt. . . . Worse still, although he perceives a slightly different slant to the writings of the Wittgensteinian group, he seems quite unaware that Wittgenstein's later philosophy is totally distinct both from logical positivism and from the ordinary-language movement. The hodge-podge of ideas, picked up from disparate sources, which Gellner attributes to the "school" he has constructed is thus not only not attributable to all members of it, but not even, taken as a whole attributable to any single member of it.

Dummett insists on the discreteness of individual philosophical statement, as well as its self-encapsulation (a motif of analytical philosophy since its early state of "logical atomism"):

> Having created a structure by picking up inconsistent bits from various sources, Gellner is able gleefully to expose the inconsistencies in that structure. He cites opposing quotations from one philosopher last year and a quite different one twenty years ago, and leaves the reader to gasp at the presumption of this school which imagines it can get away with such flagrant self-contradiction.

Whatever the defects of Gellner's volume, for our purposes here Dummett's strictures are of prime interest for his radical denial of the principle of cultural cohesion; fragmentation is not only acknowledged but raised to a virtue.

It is a virtue that, in terms of the larger cultural situation of our day, is first of all a necessity. Though a great deal more is known now than in the past, it is not known by any person. The encyclopedias record more facts, the computers catalogue more data, the libraries shelve more volumes, but individuals know proportionately less and less. Under a headline in the *New York Times* for 25 February 1985 that reads "Torrent of Print Strains the Fabric of Libraries," the librarian of Yale University is quoted as saying, "We're drowning in information and starving for knowledge." "In no other period of human knowledge," declared Max Scheler as long ago as 1928,

> has man ever become more problematic to himself than in our own days. We have a scientific, a philosophical, and a theological anthropology that know nothing of each other. Therefore we no longer possess any clear and consistent idea of man. The evergrowing multiplicity of the particular sciences that are engaged in the study of men has much more confused and obscured than elucidated our concept of man.

Ernst Cassirer, who quoted this statement late in the second quarter of the twentieth century, had, beginning in 1906, devoted a vast study to the historical evolutions of the *Erkenntnisproblem*— the problem of knowledge—which reached three volumes by 1920 and four by 1950. He attempted to counter the increasing disintegration of knowledge by his *Philosophie der symbolischen Formen* of the 1920s, but when he restated his position in his *Essay on Man* (written in English in 1944), the fragmentation of forms seemed ever more threatening:

> . . . our wealth of facts is not necessarily a wealth of thoughts. Unless we succeed in finding a clue of Ariadne to lead us out of this labyrinth, we can have no real insight into the general character of human culture; we shall remain lost in a mass of disconnected and disintegrated data which seem to lack all conceptual unity.

That the fragmentation is real, and not just a temporary realignment of cultural convention, is perhaps more dramatically realized by those teaching at the university level than by anyone else. Teachers at that level find that they can no longer assume any common body of knowledge whatever, especially among their students entering from secondary school. References to Gauss or Rousseau are met with the same puzzlement or blank incomprehension as references to Milton or Schopenhauer.

On the graduate level, a complementary witness is the vast upsurge of interest in literary or other cultural theory. Throngs enroll to hear the obscurities of Derrida or de Man; little study groups assemble to discuss the perplexities of Bakhtin or Benjamin. That few students are really good at theory seems to matter not a whit, nor does it appear to matter that much of recent theory—at least that associated with the French—has been notably nihilistic. Students seem to crave theoretical assurance the way the slaves of the Roman Empire craved the Christian message. With the latter situation, the controlling reason, one surmises, was the burden of existence; with the contemporary example, the controlling reason is surely the fragmentational chaos of modern culture. If one can get back to beginnings, seems the hope, if one can retrograde to origins, then perhaps the shards and fragments that litter the fields of culture can be intellectually restructured into coherence.

It was not always thus. When students had a common heritage in Latin literature, references to Horace and Virgil bound the group together; there seemed little need for theory, and in literary studies theory did not flourish. Even as recently as that late–nineteenth-century elite comprised by the Cambridge Apostles (my knowledge of the group is largely based on the accounts in Paul Levy, *Moore: G. E. Moore and the Cambridge Apostles* and in Victor Lowe, *Alfred North Whitehead: The Man and His Work*), a shared education in the classics preempted the need for theory; therefore, despite their frequently distinguished later contributions to the intellectual world, the Apostles developed only rudimentary conceptions in cultural theory. But now references to Horace and Virgil for the most part mean something only to specialists in Latin literature, and others have to seek elsewhere for the sense of bonding. They flock to theory, and to oblige them, theorists are springing up on all sides, their function, like that of shamans in primitive society, to mediate and control the realm of the unknown for the anxious many.

But the theorists themselves do not control forms of culture any longer. Not long ago I attended a lecture by a scholar-critic impressively introduced as an outstanding "narratologist" (the ever-narrowing specialization itself proclaims a shape of culture), who proceeded to talk in a sophisticated way of the significance of grammatical tense—the interaction of present, past, and future—in Proust. I happened to be among those who had dinner with the speaker afterwards, and, to generate polite conversation, I asked her how her theories related to the philosophical field of tense logic, specifically to Johan van Benthem's book on that topic and to Johan A. W. Kamp's monograph on "now." It turned out that she had not heard of these works; further questions made it evident that she had not heard of those philosophers either; and eventually I began to understand that she was unaware of the very existence of tense logic. And yet within the specialization of "narratology," she had an international reputation as an authority on tense. In other words, she had no command of the form of culture that would have been encompassed by her interest; her work took place exclusively as a shape of culture. Since the audience for "narratology" also made no demand for philosophical tense logic, her specialty precisely illustrated the truth that though forms of culture must relate to other forms, shapes of culture do not relate to other shapes.

Another anecdote may serve to widen the point. I was fortunate enough a few years ago to be a resident "humanist" at the Center for Advanced Study in the Behavioral Sciences at Stanford. It was an exhilarating sojourn, not least for the entirely different light it cast upon my own intellectual world. The movers and shakers of my world, the names that I and my confreres invoke and discuss, meant exactly nothing to the sociologists, psychologists, anthropologists, lawyers, linguists, logicians, and philosophers who were my colleagues. They themselves referred to different hierarchies of achievement and invoked different presumptions of value. At formal seminars we would read one another papers from our work in progress, and when those papers happened to go out of their own sphere their reception was fascinating. I happened to read a paper that had a bit to do with German philosophy of the early nineteenth century; the philosophers in my audience reacted with the uninterested tolerance and friendly perplexity with which they would have greeted a lecture on cuneiform inscriptions from Babylonian ruins. On the other hand, an eminent philosopher gave a theoretical paper on certain aspects of literary criticism, and when other philosophers asked me what I thought of it, I praised it in the same polite but abstracted way. Finally, one of them tried to pin me down, and I was forced to respond that "it was really very interesting, but it's not what anybody would do who's in the field—it just doesn't relate."

The radical unawareness of the participants in one shape of culture for the concerns and even the existence of other shapes of culture is endemic. Bruner, for instance, comments of present-day Oxford that "the fact is, one realizes after a few years, there is no Oxford, only Oxfords. Its complexities and privacies are so entrenched that established members of the place may each live in a world that overlaps only slightly with the Oxford of somebody a hundred yards away." And he supplies from his own experience an especially vivid example of this nonrelational encapsulation: "A distinguished professor of literature, encountered at tea one day, had never until that moment heard of Professor Tinbergen, though they had inhabited the place jointly for fifteen years. She was pleased to learn that he had just won a Nobel Prize."

The fragmentation is accelerating. In the second half of the nineteenth century, Emerson deplored the exponential increase in books:

> We look over with a sigh the monumental libraries of Paris, of the Vatican and the British Museum. In 1858, the number of printed books in the Imperial Library at Paris was estimated at eight hundred thousand volumes, with an annual increase of twelve thousand volumes; so that the number of printed books extant to-day may easily exceed a million. It is easy to count the number of pages which a diligent man can read in a day, and the number of years which human life in favorable circumstances allows to reading; and to demonstrate that though he should read from dawn till dark, for sixty years, he must die in the first alcoves.

Yet now, little more than a century later, the Library of Congress has something in the neighborhood of twenty million volumes on its shelves. About eight hundred thousand new volumes are published worldwide each year. The Harvard University Library subscribes to over ninety thousand periodicals. One can scarcely read the reviews, let alone the books themselves, even of elite works deemed important enough for notice by such cultural clearinghouses as the *New York Review of Books* or *TLS*.

And yet culture does not collapse. One used to hear, in those years when the premier and ministers of the French government were constantly changing, that despite the volatility of the elected leadership, the country was held together by the stability of its civil service. Such, mutatis mutandis, is the situation with regard to culture. The forms of culture are collapsing under multiplicity, and seen from the expectation of a unity of knowledge, the situation is one of hopeless fragmentation. But forms of culture are more and more tending to be empty rubrics. Knowledge is now being transacted mostly in terms of shapes of culture.

To be sure, forms have not entirely collapsed. At present, most manifestations of culture are perceived not solely as shape or as form, but shiftingly and ambiguously as part form and part shape. For instance, most devotees of painting are lured to museums only by a vague and generalized respect for culture; they experience individual paintings entirely as shapes: a painting by, say, Giorgione is viewed in an isolated moment as an encapsulated entity. The curator of Renaissance painting in the museum, however, experiences the same painting in a connected network of knowledge about other paintings by Giorgione and about the Venetian School of painting, and in a larger network about the history and styles of the Italian Renaissance in general. To that extent he experiences the Giorgione within a form of culture. More and more, though, the experience of the viewer who must see the painting as a shape of culture displaces the experience of the viewer able to see it as an element in a form of culture. Even the privileged curator's expertise in forms of culture is severely limited; his own form, Renaissance painting, itself becomes a shape when taken in the context of painting as an aesthetic category, for he cannot view a painting of, let us say, French Impressionism with equivalent connections (formally) to those with which he views the Giorgione, though he may appreciate a Monet aesthetically (as a shape) as deeply as he appreciates a Giorgione. Manifestations of culture are perceived by some as form, by most as shapes; but in general the forms are becoming more and more fragmented and constricted, and the shapes are increasing enormously.

One must be aware, however, that one aspect of the cultural scene, that defined by specialization in a science, is not usually subject to the explosion of form into shapes. Science is progressive; art is not. Paradoxically, though, the progression of science is not accompanied by accumulation, while the arts, precisely because they are not progressive, accumulate enormously. Any aspect of a science, as of an art, that accumulates will eventually change from form to shapes. But science as such maintains itself, to use the phrase now in vogue, as a "cutting edge" of knowledge. A mathematician or physicist at the age of twenty-two, for instance, can be at the frontier of his or her special interest; a student of the Italian Renaissance would be the veriest tyro at that same age. But the other side of this coin is that nothing of humanistic culture ever becomes obsolete, and almost everything of science becomes wholly irrelevant as it is displaced by new knowledge. For example, the interests of literary and intellectual history sustain the whole of the work of Dryden, which occupies many volumes in scholarly editions, as an object of concern; Dryden's contemporary, Sir Robert Boyle, who was in no wise culturally less important, is remembered by science only for Boyle's law, which can be expressed in a single line of type in any text.

This ruthless winnowing to keep sharp a cutting edge is the very essence of scientific progress. Laplace, to cite an example, is admired as one of the very greatest of astronomers and as "one of the finest mathematicians in history"; a study of the progress of astronomy called *The Discovery of Our Galaxy*, however, where this phrase occurs, indicates that almost all of Laplace's mighty and voluminous endeavors have now been modified or displaced, and there is apparently not even the unqualified single line of a Boyle's law to represent him at the cutting edge of astronomy. For example, Laplace almost but not quite foresaw black holes: "A luminous star of the density of the earth, and having a diameter two hundred and fifty times that of the sun would not, by virtue of its gravitational attraction, let any of its light escape to us. Thus, it is possible that the largest luminous bodies of the universe are, for that very reason, invisible." But to this the astronomer Charles Whitney, who writes from the cutting edge of modern science, replies:

> Laplace's statement, that a monstrous star with the density of the earth and 250 times the diameter of the sun would not be seen, is in itself a monstrosity—no star like that could be formed of matter as we know it. . . . Interestingly enough, the General Theory of Relativity does imply that bodies might be invisible as a consequence of gravity, although they would have a much higher density than Laplace's star.

This radical discarding of what is not current and relevant to the concerns of the frontier makes sciences at their cutting edge exempt from the form-to-shape metamorphosis; such cutting edges are constituted neither as form nor as shape, although the vast mass of discarded material, as the history of science, does fall into the categories of other cultural manifestations. An anecdote might serve to show how manageable the cutting edge itself is, however. A party to honor the birthday of the physicist S. B. Treiman at Princeton University was reported this way:

> Four Nobel Prize winning physicists spoke at Physics Department Chairman Sam Treiman's 60th birthday celebration. . . . Professors David Gross and Curtis Callan threw the party, and its theme was "The Weak Interactions: Past, Present and Future."
>
> The four prize winners were Val Fitch of Princeton, T. D. Lee of Columbia, James Cronin of Chicago, and Steven Weinberg *57 of Texas. Fitch and Cronin worked together at Princeton before Cronin went to Chicago. Lee was at the Institute for Advanced Study. . . . And Weinberg was Treiman's graduate student.
>
> The other two speakers at the all-day conference were Abraham Pais of Rockefeller University . . . and Leon Lederman, director of Fermi National Laboratory. . . . Last year Treiman won the Oersted Medal, an award that . . . was given . . . for

the first time in recognition of Treiman's work with graduate students. . . .

"I like students," says Treiman, "and I've had some very good ones, and I like doing science. It's been a rewarding life. I've been lucky to live in exciting times—discoveries and developments bubbling up through my whole lifetime. There have been enormous accomplishments.

"It's a pity more people don't follow physics. It's a little technical, but really no more difficult to learn than French. And the subject is humane, contrary to popular conceptions. The objects we study are not human, but the work itself is very collegial. We build on each other; our work is part of a long historical chain. Though physics is an old, honorable subject, it has simply exploded in this century, with quantum mechanics, relativity, particle physics, solid state physics and more. It's exciting now . . . right here in this University . . . upstairs!"

The cutting edge of a science, as indicated in Treiman's happy report, is subject to the explosion of its antecedent forms but is not inundated by their sequent debris as shapes; for the winnowing of the irrelevant constantly keeps the knowledge manageable. Moreover, the cutting edge of a science is directed eventually toward a technology, and technology does not have much to do with culture. To understand this truth, it is only necessary to think of one of those utopian projections into the future cast in terms of extreme technological advancement. Such brave new worlds are always depressing, no matter how gleaming their technology. Why are they so invariably and without exception melancholy? Because, one surmises, though they have technology, they have no culture. Technologically futuristic worlds are worlds that are posited without a vision of culture, and culture alone pursues meaning. As a consequence such worlds always seem inhuman and uncanny. "There is no such thing," suggests Clifford Geertz, "as a human nature independent of culture."

Except, therefore, for the continual refocussings associated with a cutting edge of science, which themselves tend away from the interests peculiar to culture, any form of culture, even one constituted by the historical study of a science, is under pressure toward the fragmentation into shapes. Such shapes are protean, and they constitute the largest part of what occupies most of our intellectual activity. Seen from the traditional hope for formal unity of knowledge, the cultural situation is a depressing ruin, and claims to knowing a kind of madness; the actual situation, however, is much less bleak. Since shapes of culture do not relate to one another, the breakdown of interrelationship brings with it no anxiety: only forms relate to integrated wholes and can thus be fragmented; shapes cohere without integration. They do not relate among themselves, nor do they imply one another. They simply float, bloblike, in our group awareness. My colleagues at the Center for Advanced Study in the Behavioral Sciences, and I myself, were not depressed; on the contrary, we had a rollicking time of partying, wine-tasting, and general conviviality. The shapes of culture that made up our varied areas of knowledge and accredited us for inclusion in such conviviality were, as structures of knowledge, like Leibniz's monads, windowless, coexisting yet not interacting, but each expressing all reality from within its own encapsulation.

The actual cultural situation is thus a benign chaos of floating shapes. Specializations contract into ever more constricted spheres, their possessors knowing that within them they can float undisturbed in generally compartmented spaces of culture, like pleasure craft at a marina. The less relationship or interconnection the specializations have, the better for their beneficiary. A cultural generalist is an oddity for whom modern intellectual society finds little use; rewards are for the specialist alone. It is actually better for such a specialist to know one thing than many things. A student of French literature who claimed authority in the Enlightenment and in the medieval period as well would find it more difficult to procure a job than one who offered merely one of the two. And the student would be entitled to triumphant ignorance in everything outside his or her specialty.

A second specialty, in truth, would be like a flange that kept the candidate from sliding with satisfying solidity into a departmental slot. A molecular biologist knows nothing about the law of contracts, and would be thought frivolous if he did. A neurologist knows nothing of the philosophy of Plato. A prima ballerina knows nothing of the mechanics of architecture. Recently I had dinner in an Oxford college with a Wordsworthian scholar, a Byzantinist, and a mathematician. Our specialties indicated our mutual social acceptability, but it is perhaps unnecessary to say that we did not talk about Wordsworth's poetry, nor about Byzantium, nor about the theory of equations.

An attractive illustration for all this may be summoned from David Lodge's comic novel, *Small World: An Academic Romance,* about a world which, as the narrator says, "resembles exactly what is sometimes called the real world, without corresponding exactly to it." The novel deals hilariously with the proliferation of conferences in contemporary cultural activity, and it presents vividly the social intermingling that accompanies the unrelated encapsulations of modern shapes of culture:

> . . . not all the conferences that are going on this summer are concerned with English literature, not by any means. There are at the same time conferences in session on French medieval *chansons* and Spanish poetic drama of the sixteenth century and the German *Sturm und Drang* movement and Serbian folksongs; there are conferences on the dynasties of ancient Crete and the social history of the Scottish Highlands and the foreign policy of Bismarck and the sociology of sport and the economic controversy over monetarism; there are conferences on low-temperature physics and microbiology and oral pathology and quasars and catastrophe theory. Sometimes, when two conferences share the same accommodation, confusions occur: it has been known for a bibliographer specializing in the history of punctuation to sit through the first twenty minutes of a medical paper on "Malfunctions of the Colon" before he realized his mistake.

> But, on the whole, academic subject groups are self-defining, exclusive entities. Each has its own jargon, pecking order, newsletter, professional association. . . . Each subject, and each conference devoted to it, is a world unto itself. . . .

Frequently shapes of culture present themselves in the mask of form. The Nobel Prize–winning biologist James Watson, in his volume *The Double Helix,* which is about the discovery of the structure of DNA, disarmingly presents himself as knowing hardly enough chemistry, crystallography, and mathematics to proceed with his investigation. The actual knowledge he summoned for his task was a kind of *bricolage,* shaped for his purpose, but scarcely participating in the formal structure of those disciplines. Indeed, that "personal knowledge," which in the influential formulation of Michael Polanyi is widely recognized as more important for the investigations of science than publicly avowed scientific methodology, is really a shape of culture as opposed to the form of a discipline.

Other masqueradings of shape under the nominal alignments of form can be identified in other regions of culture. For instance, though in the Edwardian era classical studies at Cambridge encapsulated themselves almost entirely as a shape of culture, classical studies at Berlin at about the same time laid claim to the historical linearity of a form of culture. Starting with F. A. Wolf in the 1790s and continuing through the nineteenth century with scholars such as August Boeckh, Gottfried Hermann, and Karl Lachmann, the Germans convinced themselves that they were engaged in a cumulative "science" (*Altertumswissenschaft*). By the first decade of the twentieth century Berlin had assembled the most remarkable group of classical scholars ever to reside at the same university (it is hard to grasp that a figure of the eminence of Johannes Vahlen was no better than seventh or eighth in the rankings that could be accorded this group). They were all under the illusion that they were engaged in a science. When Gilbert Murray introduced himself to Wilamowitz by a letter written in elegant Attic Greek, the titan of German scholarship struck up a cordial acquaintance, but confided to his memoirs that Murray was "not a scientist."

In Wilamowitz's commitment to the historical linearity of "science," despite the actual self-referential encapsulation of classical studies, it was as though he hallucinated a formal parallelogram within the amorphous ellipse of the cultural shape. But it was scarcely more than a game. Indeed, his younger colleague and successor to his chair, Werner Jaeger, in effect inscribed another ellipse within the parallelogram, for Jaeger treated classical studies as a flowering from a single intuition about Greek culture. In a memorial speech on

Jaeger by that scholar's colleague and successor at Berlin, Wolfgang Schadewalt, Wilamowitz is characterized as an "expansive" scholar, that is, one who tried systematically to expand his knowledge to cover the entire field of classical learning. Jaeger, on the other hand, is characterized as an "architectonic" scholar; that is, he had an intuition of his total position from the first, and his subsequent achievement filled in the details of this initial vision. But the initial vision itself, that of the centrality of *paideia* in Greek civilization, was, though Schadewalt of course does not use the phrase, a shape of culture.

That culture can subsist in shapes despite the breakdown of its forms can be realized from a consideration of one of the characteristics of shape noted earlier. Though forms when overloaded or stunted break off into shapes and in that sense seem to decline into shapes, shapes are not necessarily, even if they can be so specifically, a deterioration of form. For shape is prior to form as well, and reality is built on shapes before it witnesses the evolution of form.

A choice example of this precedence is supplied in an anecdote by the great chemist Justus Liebig, about the status of chemistry before it became a recognized form of culture (a form that owed much to the efforts of Liebig himself):

> . . . my position at school was very deplorable . . . languages and everything that is acquired by their means, that gains praise and honor in the school, were out of my reach; and when the venerable rector of the gymnasium (Zimmermann), on one occasion of his examination of my class, came to me and made a most cutting remonstrance with me for my want of diligence, how I was the plague of my teacher and the sorrow of my parents, and what did I think was to become of me, and when I answered him that I would be a chemist, the whole school and the good old man himself broke into an uncontrollable fit of laughter, for no one at the time had any idea that chemistry was a thing that could be studied.

When Liebig advanced to university level, he found that "at most of the universities there was no special chair for chemistry; it was generally handed over to the professor of medicine, who taught it, as much as he knew of it, and that was little enough, along with the branches of toxicology, pharmacology, materia medica, practical medicine, and pharmacy."

That the priority of shape to form accounts for the viability of culture even after its forms have been shattered does not, however, account for the viability of the shapes in themselves. To understand how they are able to maintain the functions of culture it will be necessary to address ourselves to certain divisions in the structure of meaning itself. These divisions are not put forward to contest any of the numerous distinctions propounded by philosophers from Frege onward; rather, for the purposes of this book's argument, they should be seen not as entries in a continuing philosophical debate but instead as primordial fault lines underlying the seamless surface of ordinary assumption.

If the present cultural situation can be compared to multitudinous sailing ships and power craft bobbing comfortably each in its own slip at the marinas constructed by English studies or chemistry, or some other nominal discipline, it is also true that the craft, no matter how different and unrelated in look and in voyage, share a common—a Platonic—form as boat. To transume the metaphor for the problem of meaning, it is as though despite the kaleidoscopic variety of meanings in modern culture, all meanings were refractions of the same primary light. Like Leibniz's monads, one shape of culture, though independent of the others, tells its participants the whole story, or at least as much of it as is necessary. After all, when Joseph Conrad, in a great instant, beholds "all the truth of life," that truth, stunningly, is merely "a moment of vision, a sigh, a smile, and the return to an eternal rest." The fundamental meanings that alone have meaning are few in number and available to all. All the others, all the structures and sophistications and arcane ramifications, are merely translations.

Should we think that Conrad's specifications, even allowing for their rhetorical status as symbols representing larger entities, too radically constrict the truths available to human life, we should at least pause to think also about the quotidian dissipations of that life. To think, that is, about how much of life is spent in daily repetitions devoid of enlightening truth. To think how much is spent in boredom, how much in daydreams and listless disconnection, how much in sleep, how much in pain, physical or psychic, how much, above all, in what Oscar Wilde calls "the same wearisome round of stereotyped habits." Though such accounting would render different balances for different people, for everyone it might suggest that the actual moments of truth are less frequently encountered, at the same time that they are more unpredictably available, than careless supposition might assume. Myriads "in a brazen prison live / . . . Their lives to some unmeaning taskwork give." In that sense, the sense in which our lives are flattened by the endless weight of the quotidian, their content supplied by the fact that the days repeat themselves, we might be more disposed toward accepting the view that the bulk of human mental activity consists in translational exchanges. We push the counters around, as it were, while the effulgent moments of actual meaning shine upon us only at unforeseen intervals.

It is the intuition that meanings that truly are meanings are sporadic in appearance, few in number, and open to all that accounts, I believe, for a persistent strain in the history of thought. This strain is openly scornful of the need or pertinence of an influx of knowledge from outside; though expressed in many and differing matrices, its statements have in common a confidence that what really needs to be known does not have to be learned. "Reynolds," says Blake, "Thinks that Man Learns all that he Knows I say on the Contrary That Man Brings All that he has or Can have Into the World with him. Man is Born Like a Garden ready Planted & Sown This World is too poor to produce one Seed." But since there is an enormous amount of knowledge that can only be learned from outside, vastly more indeed than anyone can ever know, the subtext of the passage must surely be that it is meaning, not knowledge as such, that dwells within.

The same insistence, from a different perspective, characterizes the thought of Leibniz:

It is a bad habit we have of thinking as if our souls received certain forms as messengers and as if it had doors and windows. We have all these forms in our minds, and even from all time, because the mind always expresses all its future thoughts and already thinks confusedly of everything of which it will ever think distinctly. Nothing can be taught us the idea of which is not already in our minds, as the matter out of which this thought is formed. This Plato has excellently recognized when he puts forward his doctrine of reminiscence. . . . Aristotle preferred to compare our souls to tablets that are still blank but upon which there is a place for writing and maintained that there is nothing in our understanding that does not come from the senses. This conforms more with popular notions, as Aristotle usually does, while Plato goes deeper.

Wordsworth, again, in a wholly different context of argument, maintains, and we perhaps have noticed as much ourselves if we have paid attention in life, that greatness of soul seems to have nothing to do with education, an influx of knowledge, or recognition by others:

> Oh! many are the Poets that are sown
> By Nature; men endowed with the highest gifts,
> The vision and the faculty divine.
>
> .   .   .   .
>
> these favoured Beings
> All but a scattered few, live out their time,
> Husbanding that which they possess within,
> And go to the grave, unthought of.

So much for the decline of cultural forms and about the fewness in number and the subjective location of meanings that are meanings. The next chapter will address the question of what is meant by meaning.

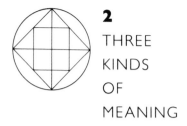

2
THREE
KINDS
OF
MEANING

The previous chapter considered the decline of cultural forms, the fact that a proliferation of commentary and new publication swells knowledge until it bulges out of its original forms and bursts into a cascade of specialist shapes. I identified this transformation as the distinctive phenomenon of the modern intellectual situation, noting that the new shapes of culture do not relate to one another and that the modern cultural scene is increasingly a benign chaos of floating shapes. Knowledge has increased so exponentially that no one can know very much of it; its forms are no longer commensurable. And yet culture does not collapse. I concluded by suggesting that shapes can carry the burden of culture because while knowledge is increasing exponentially, meaning does not increase at all. In fact, I suggested that meaning is always in short supply, and that its full range is both severely restricted and available to all; that therefore the isolated shapes, which carry all available meanings, support all the necessary interests of culture. By this argument, knowledge and the forms by which it is organized, whatever the conventional assumptions about them, are not essential to culture, but meaning is.

These are hard words about knowledge and about the forms of culture by which knowledge is organized, fighting words, perhaps, and they call for more justification than can be given them here. I shall here merely point out that knowledge accumulates in the world as a whole and constantly changes in individuals, but that culture is not progressive. The triumphs of culture bear only a slight ratio to the advancement of knowledge; much more is known today than was known in fifth-century Athens, but culture is not superior today to culture in fifth-century Athens. So too with respect to quattrocento Florence or Elizabethan London. Science advances; culture waxes and wanes but does not advance. Meaning, which directs culture, does not advance either and does not depend on knowledge. As a single paradoxical example, Leibniz, whose encyclopedic knowledge is one of the wonders of intellectual history, in effect discounts all that mighty attainment by saying, as was quoted at the conclusion of the previous chapter, that "it is a bad habit we have of thinking as if our souls received certain forms as messengers and as if it had doors and windows. We have all these forms in our minds, and even from all time." Whatever else he may have been saying, he was saying that all necessary meanings are independent of knowledge, as was Augustine when he counseled: "Noli foras ire, in te redi, in interiore homine habitat veritas"—"Do not seek to go out; go back into yourself; truth dwells in the inner man."

Though knowledge seems to have little to do with meaning, actually the two are not wholly without connection, even if that connection has historically been tenuous to the point almost of nonexistence. Doubtless if knowledge ever accumulated to a certain point, meanings would finally change. In history so far, however, there has not been enough augmentation of knowledge to affect the store of meaning, and the lack of apparent relevance is compounded by the fact that individuals have at their command only a tiny and indeed ever shrinking portion of knowledge, though they can at least in principle experience the totality of meaning.

Obviously, a very heavy burden is being placed on the conception of meaning, and the reader has every right to ask me what I mean by meaning. I shall try in this chapter to answer that urgent question, but the answer, like so much of what I am contending, will be encased in paradox. Though philosophers, particularly in this century, like to talk about meaning, frequently formulate descriptions of meaning, disagree about meaning, and love nothing better than to deny meaning to the statements of others, their lucubrations hardly help the situation. We all know what we mean by meaning, even if we find it difficult to say what that is. We will let no philosopher's definition evict our sense of what meaning is, and we go merrily through life, or somberly, as the case may be, without worrying about the definition of meaning.

Except for me. I have maneuvered myself into the position where I must stand and deliver on a definition of meaning. It is a hazardous prospect. I can expect little quarter from philosophers, whom I have just been abusing, and in any event my own theories indicate that what they say could hardly relate to the shape of my cultural discourse. I know what I mean by meaning, however, and I shall try to persuade my readers to concur in the meaning of my meaning. Though I developed my own opinions inductively, I shall present them as stipulative assertions.

There are two, and only two, publicly accessible kinds of meaning. We may call them *meaning by experience* and *meaning by equivalence*. Russell has of course influentially propounded a dichotomy that may initially sound somewhat similar; but the similarity is more apparent than real, and as this argument will proceed in quite different directions from his, it seems best to invoke a terminology suited for the purpose, even at the risk of sounding derivative.

Meaning by experience is only a small part of what we know, but it is also the absolute to which all other meanings are referred. Indeed, when we use the word *meaning* as something in itself, it is meaning by experience to which we refer. Meaning by equivalence, on the other hand, is overwhelmingly the substance of culture. All education proceeds by analogical incrementations of our primary experience, and its expansion of meaning is always a meaning by equivalence. If, for example, I encounter a word I do not know, say, *ineluctable,* and I ask its meaning, that meaning is always given as an equivalence. I look into a dictionary and find that *ineluctable,* which I do not know, means the equivalent of *unavoidable,* which I do know, not from a dictionary but by its invocation in contexts of my primary experience.

We broaden our knowledge by minute incrementations that are versions of inexact synonymy. "All thinking is analogizing," urges Emerson, "and it is the use of life to learn metonymy." ("Every one knows," says Berkeley in the fourth dialogue of *Alciphron,* "that *analogy* is a Greek word used by mathematicians to signify a similitude of proportions. For instance, when we observe that two is to six as three is to nine, this similitude or equality of proportion is termed analogy. And, although proportion strictly signifies the habitude or relation of one quantity to another, yet, in a looser and translated sense, it hath been applied to signify every other habitude; and consequently, the term *analogy* comes to signify all similitude of relations or habitudes whatsoever.") For instance Bacon, as was suggested in the previous chapter, did not know China by experience; as an encyclopedist, however, he could have a satisfactory knowledge of China by equivalence. He, like any of us, could simply make metonymic substitutions. (Berkeley, in the seventh dialogue of *Alciphron,* argues that "all sciences" depend on a process of substitution: "the mind . . . seems naturally led to substitute. . . . Nothing, I say, is more natural than to make the things we know a step toward those we do not know; and to explain and represent things less familiar by others which are more so.")

Thus with Bacon: he knew what a realm was, for he had experienced England and could equate that experience, by minute variations, with the realm of China. He did not know the emperor of China but he knew the King of England, and he could read Marco Polo and equate Kublai Khan, by inexact synonymy (or proportional analogy), with James the First. He knew by experience what hills, valleys, and rivers were; what men and women were; what town and country were; what food and drink were—and all these he could translate, by incremental analogy, into a knowledge of the situation in China. All our education, both that of the classroom and that provided by the course of life itself, is metonymic; it proceeds by the analogical incrementations of meaning by equivalence. All our education is a kind of translation.

Meaning by equivalence accounts for the overwhelming preponderance of what we know. Perhaps ninety-nine percent of what we know, in truth, has its meaning by equivalence and thereby by translation. I look around my study as I write this sentence and see perhaps three thousand books lining its walls and that of the adjacent room; every single one in some way translates the meaning I gain from experience into a meaning by equivalence.

Meaning by experience, though it be, by the percentage put forward, restricted to perhaps only one part in a hundred of what we know, is paradoxically not even that large for everyone. For meaning by experience is itself cast into two forms, *primary meaning* and *transcendent meaning,* and it seems that not all people experience the second form. (One would prefer another word than *transcendent,* but it both fits the situation and is charged with significance from prior usage, so *transcendent* the word must remain.)

Primary meaning is a version of perception itself, and without it we cannot live our lives: it is the knowledge of the desk in front of me, of the fire in the hearth, of the tree outside the window. If it be objected that the "knowledge" of the "tree outside the window" does not seem to address the problem of "meaning," the response is that the request for a meaning, as distinguished from meaning as such, is always the request for a meaning by equivalence. Primary meanings are not meanings by equivalence but meanings by experience. The meaning of the tree is the perception of the tree.

This contention, though not without prefiguration, runs radically counter to dominant currents of modern thought, as seen, for a single instance, in Michael Dummett's rebuke of Frege: "Meaning, under any theory whatever, cannot be *in principle* subjective, because meaning is a matter of what is *conveyed* by language." But what Dummett refers to as meaning—his position is adapted from the later Wittgenstein, the so-called "private language argument"— is meaning by equivalence. Indeed, meaning takes place in the *understanding* of language or experience, and that can happen only within an individual mind. It would follow that meaning as such must always be "in principle subjective." (In a related apprehension, Oscar Wilde insists that "all artistic creation is absolutely subjective. The very landscape that Corot looked at was, as he said himself, but a mood of his own mind. . . . For out of ourselves we can never pass.")

The meaning of the tree is the perception of the tree. If the tree then be called an "arbre" or a "Baum" a meaning by equivalence is being added; indeed, to call it a "tree" is itself a meaning by equivalence. A tree could not have primary meaning for someone born and brought up on Mars. By the same token, the experience of a multiplicity of trees does not augment the primary meaning of tree, although a forest is its own primary experience. But only one experience in a category can be primary. All secondary experience has meaning by equivalence.

The matter is extraordinarily important. Almost all meanings inhere in the invocation of something else; almost all are meanings by equivalence. But if there is a meaning that is a meaning, it must inhere in itself alone (for meaning by equivalence in a sense denies meaning as such). That is the nature of meaning by experience, which is a conception closer to Heidegger's view of meaning as disclosure of being (see *Sein und Zeit*, secs. 32, 44, 65) than to the assumptions of analytical philosophy.

Understandings by experience are truths that bear their own meanings. As Spinoza says, "sane sicut lux seipsam et tenebras manifestat, sic veritas norma sui, et falsi est"—"even as light illuminates both itself and darkness, so is truth the standard both of itself and of falsity." Take the color red, which was asserted in the previous chapter to be unavailable to mathematical description. If the color red is not experienced, no description or equivalence can supply its meaning. I remember once coming to a friend's apartment. When he opened the door I saw that something had changed. We were young and impoverished, and he was living in a faculty apartment that was rented unfurnished. The walls were a kind of hideous tomato-soup pink, with high ceilings and beautiful walnut-lined windows. But I blanched when I saw what the change was: my friend had been over to the next town and bought cheap plastic draperies for the windows; they were dark green, and the effect with the walls was bizarre. He looked at me proudly and said, "What do you think?" I replied, as tactfully as possible, "Very nice. But I should have thought red drapes might be better." He looked at me with perplexity and said: "They *are* red." Nothing would convince him, and I was reduced to going out and stopping some students on the street to bear witness to the non-redness of my friend's drapes. Either one knows red by primary experience, or one does not know it at all.

That, indeed, is the conclusion that John Locke urges, using the same color red:

And therefore he that has not before received into his Mind, by the proper Inlet, the simple *Idea* which any Word stands for, can never come to know the signification of that Word, by any other Words, or Sounds, whatsoever put together, according to any Rules or Definition. . . . A studious blind Man, who had mightily beat his Head about visible Objects, and made use of the explication of his Books and Friends, to understand those names of Light, and Colours, which often came in his way; bragg'd one day, That he now understood what *Scarlet* signified. Upon which his Friend demanding, what *Scarlet* was? the blind Man answered, it was like the Sound of a Trumpet. Just such an Understanding of the name of any other simple *Idea* will he have, who hopes to get it only from a Definition, or other Words made use of to explain it.

Locke goes on to say:

He that should use the word *Rainbow,* to one who knew all those Colours, but yet had never seen that *Phænomenon,* would, by enumerating the Figure, Largeness, Position, and Order of the Colours, so well define that word, that it might be perfectly understood. But yet that *Definition,* how exact and perfect soever, would never make a blind Man understand it; because several of the simple Ideas that make that complex one, being such as he never received by Sensation and Experience, no words are able to excite them in his Mind.

The color red can only be known by experience, and to know it by experience is exactly to understand it as a meaning. Wittgenstein, in his *Philosophical Investigations,* repeatedly invokes the color red in argumentation about fundamentals of knowledge and meaning, and his views accord with this asseveration: "when I want to explain the word 'red' to someone in the sentence 'That is not red,' I do it by pointing to something red" (par. 429); "saying that the word 'red' 'refers to' instead of 'means' something private does not help us in the least to grasp its function" (par. 274—and see further pars. 1, 30n., 53, 57, 58, 313).

Everyone initially composes his or her world by primary meanings, and everyone experiences these meanings. It does not seem to follow, however, that everyone also experiences transcendent meanings, which are in any event far more rare in their occurrence, even for those who do experience them. Such meanings, indeed, appear to be mainly associated with two deep lodes of human experience.

The first lode is the sexuality of men and women, and the diamonds of transcendence sometimes to be gathered there are called love, more specifically first love or at least the first of love. Though such transcendence is inseparable from sexuality, it is not precisely sexuality as such. Sexuality as such is in rich supply in life, but the transcendent meaning called love is experienced only briefly if at all. Much and even most eroticism, even intense eroticism, does not, despite its pleasure, participate in meaning. We can readily verify this fact either by consulting our own experience or by calling to mind any of the numerous expressions in common speech, such as "one-night stand," that indicate that sexual transport in itself is not a locus of meaning. But love is. Love is a transcendent meaning, even though that meaning is evanescent, severely restricted in time, and not experienced by all—"Deep as first love, and wild with all regret; / O Death in Life, the days that are no more!"

When love is experienced, however, life suddenly becomes transfigured; it becomes whole and good:

> I wonder, by my troth, what thou and I
> Did, till we loved? Were we not weaned till then,
> But sucked on country pleasures, childishly?
>
> .   .   .   .
>
> And now good morrow to our waking souls,
> Which watch not one another out of fear;
> For love all love of other sights controls,
> And makes one little room an everywhere.

Donne's lines bear direct witness, as do innumerable other statements in the annals of culture. But even in the sardonic rumination of Nietzsche the sense of love as true meaning can be discerned as an antithetical intertext in an ironic statement:

> Do you desire the most astonishing proof of how far the transfiguring power of intoxication can go? "Love" is this proof: that which is called love in all the languages and silences of the world. In this case, intoxication has done with reality to

such a degree that in the consciousness of the lover the cause of it is extinguished and something else seems to have taken its place—a vibration and glittering of all the magic mirrors of Circe—. . . . And in any case, one lies well when one loves . . . one seems to oneself transfigured, stronger, richer, more perfect, one *is* more perfect— Here we discover *art* as an organic function: we discover it in the most angelic instinct, "love"; we discover it as the greatest stimulus of life—art thus sublimely expedient even when it lies—

But we should do wrong if we stopped with its power to lie: it does more than merely imagine; it even transposes values: the lover *is* more valuable, is stronger. . . . His whole economy is richer than before, more powerful, more *complete* than in those who do not love. . . . If we subtracted all traces of this intestinal fever from lyricism in sound and word, what would be left of lyrical poetry and music?—*L'art pour l'art* perhaps: the virtuoso croaking of shivering frogs, despairing in their swamp— All the rest was created by love—

A second lode of experience that casts up transcendent meaning is associated with childhood. The transcendent meaning sometimes encountered in these environs is of a generative importance to culture at least equal to that of love, though it seems to be rarer in its appearance, or at least limited to the experience of a smaller number of people. We may call this form of transcendence "Wordsworthian" meaning to differentiate it from the transcendence called love. It is not, however, by any means restricted to the Wordsworthian situation. Nevertheless, it is so rare and evanescent that it will be difficult to indicate satisfactorily, and the attempt will necessarily entail a lengthier invocation than that accorded love. Furthermore, the invocation will be forced to rely on the memory of personal experience that others might not share, as well as on selected passages that occur in public culture.

The first such passage, fittingly drawn from Wordsworth himself, is the immortal skating scene from the first book of *The Prelude*. If one asks what the skating scene means, a meaning by equivalence can be supplied, but such meaning is mundane. The transcendent meaning, however, is tremendous and ineffable. Either one has had the transcendent experience the lines report or one has not; it is a kind of judging of elect and nonelect to ask others whether they surge with the wonder and ecstasy of the lines, for some do not.

> So through the darkness and the cold we flew
> And not a voice was idle; with the din
> Smitten, the precipices rang aloud;
> The leafless trees and every crag
> Tinkled like iron; while far distant hills
> Into the tumult sent an alien sound
> Of melancholy not unnoticed, while the stars
> Eastward were sparkling clear, and in the west
> The orange sky of evening died away.

In the third kind of meaning, nothing unusual happens, something just is. What is, is being; not the becoming of equivalence, but being itself. It is almost commonplace to realize that "the stars / Eastward were sparkling clear, and in the west / The orange sky of evening died away." But the statement is unspeakably intense. In a true apprehending of these lines, which can occur only by drawing on the memory of personal experience of the third kind of meaning, one understands them as containing all there is; all there need be; all there should be. They present being.

But this sounds banal. One tries, lamely, by descriptive equivalence to evoke a meaning already defined as untranslatable and unequivalent. It cannot be evoked. One problem is that transcendent meaning is in no cognitive way different from primary meaning; it differs only by an intensity and clarity felt, not thought, and encapsulated in the subject. For instance, the primary meaning of the tree outside the window is open to all; its transcendent meaning is disclosed only to some. "The tree which moves some to tears of joy," observes Blake, "is in the Eyes of others only a Green thing that stands in the way." "I don't know how one can walk by a tree and not be happy at the sight of it," says Dostoevsky's Prince Myshkin. ("I have made the capital mistake all my life," wrote Hazlitt, "in imagining that those objects which lay open to all . . . spoke a common language to all. . . . Not so. The vital air, the sky, the woods, the streams—all these go for nothing, except with a favoured few.")

Yet, though transcendent meaning is precisely congruent in structure with primary meaning, and therefore, by the principle of the identity of indiscernibles, impossible to describe, it can, by analogy with the subjective certainty of one who has experienced it, at least be pointed out. Emerson is testifying to transcendent meaning when he says: "Crossing a bare common, in snow puddles, at twilight, under a clouded sky, without having in my thoughts any occurrence of special good fortune, I have enjoyed a perfect exhilaration. I am glad to the brink of fear."

Emerson realizes that primary meaning, open and unavoidable for all, is not the same as this transcendent meaning, this third kind of meaning, open to all but not experienced by all: "Most persons do not see the sun. At least they have a very superficial seeing. The sun illuminates only the eye of the man, but shines into the eye and the heart of the child." It shone into Wordsworth's heart:

> Daily the common range of visible things
> Grew dear to me: already I began
> To love the sun; a boy I loved the sun,
> Not as I since have loved him, as a pledge
> And surety of our earthly life, a light
> Which we behold and feel we are alive;
> Nor for his bounty to so many worlds—
> But for this cause, that I had seen him lay
> His beauty on the morning hills, had seen
> The western mountain touch his setting orb,
> In many a thoughtless hour, when from excess
> Of happiness, my blood appeared to flow
> For its own pleasure, and I breathed with joy.

It is in childhood that transcendent meanings are most accessible, at least to those for whom they are accessible at all. Since certainty in this matter can rest only upon personal experience, I shall report, as fully as I can remember it, one such experience that filled me with ecstasy not only at the time, but for many years afterward. But nothing happened, at least nothing that any outer observer could have taken as significant. What did happen was an inner experience of total completeness, radiant clarity, and absolute coherence. I was a child, perhaps as young as four but more probably somewhere between six and eight. We had finished supper, but it was still twilight, and fireflies were glowing outside. I went outdoors and down the hill to the second house below us. Adults—they were actually boys and girls of fifteen or sixteen, as I remember—were sitting on the porch in the twilight. I went up the steps and over to the side of the porch, which overhung the next house down the hill by perhaps a dozen or fifteen feet. I looked over the side of the porch, conscious of the hum of the conversation behind me, and onto the lawn below with its fireflies and the bushes surrounding it. There in the twilight I knew and understood all existence. All being was open to me. For many, many years afterward—I no longer do so—I would think of that moment and experience a flood of joy.

Although my own experience of the third kind of meaning was ineffable, I can descry analogies to it in the formulations of other cultural figures. What I experienced had much in common with many evocations in Wordsworth, especially those "renovating" moments that he called "spots of time," and with the intensities presented in such profusion in the first two books of *The Prelude*. Again, what I experienced seems to bear at least partial analogy to what Joyce called "epiphanies," which were the "revelation of the whatness of a thing," an experience in which "the soul of the commonest object . . . seems to us radiant." As Richard Ellmann notes, "the more eloquent epiphanies . . . often portray the accession of a sudden joy."

Testimonials to the third kind of meaning, and analogies to my own experience, are also presented in the twenty "anamnetische Experimente" that Eric Voegelin sets forth in his *Anamnesis: Zur Theorie der Geschichte und Politik*. They are all concerned with the "Erfahrung von der Transzendenz des Bewusstseins"—"experience of the transcendence of consciousness"—and are "Erfahrungen, die zur Besinnung treiben und die deshalb treiben, weil sie das Bewusstsein zu Existenzschauern erregt haben"—"experiences that force reflection, and do so because they have awakened consciousness to the wonder of existence." One of them, "Die Köln-Düsseldorfer," may be quoted to show how close they can be to my own experience of the third kind of meaning:

> The Cologne-Düsseldorf boats were the great and festive world. They were colored white and light yellow. . . . During the summer, organized groups rented such boats. One then saw them coming up the river at night, turn around at Bonn, and then coming down again. On the decks were Chinese lanterns, music, and dancing people. It was a magic world sliding past, strange and mysterious; intimations of something intoxicating but unknown.

Here, as in my own experience, nothing very significant to an uninvolved observer seems to happen. The boat goes up the river, turns around, and goes back down. But to Voegelin it was "a magic world sliding past," with "intimations" of Wordsworthian intensity.

It is unusual for a formal thinker like Voegelin to take note of the third kind of meaning. To lyric sensibilities, however, poets and novelists, such meaning is at the forefront of their awareness, even if not identified by specific nomenclature. For an example virtually at random, in an interview in the *New York Times* for Thursday, November 21, 1985, John Updike says in passing that "in all of our childhoods we are open to experience in a way we cease to be," and later he observes that "you use up those first 20 years of your life one way or another, and the material you collect in adulthood doesn't have that—it's not that magical."

Although the nonerotic or "Wordsworthian" experience of the third kind of meaning seems, as Updike notes, to be concentrated in childhood, as are most of the examples brought forward by Voegelin, the youth is often on his way attended by the vision splendid, and though at length for the man it dies away, and fades into the light of common day, even in adulthood there are occasional though infrequent transcendent experiences of meaning. De Quincey reports one to which Wordsworth attested in conversation:

> Just now [said Wordsworth], my ear was placed upon the stretch, in order to catch any sound of wheels that might come down

upon the lake of Wythburn from the Keswick road; at the very instant when I raised my head from the ground, in final abandonment of hope for this night, at the very instant when the organs of attention were all at once relaxing from their tension, the bright star hanging in the air above those outlines of massy brightness fell suddenly upon my eye, and penetrated my capacity of apprehension with a pathos and a sense of the infinite, that would not have arrested me under any other circumstances.

I too have experienced transcendent meaning in years advanced beyond childhood, though less frequently and comprehensively later than earlier. An example from my young manhood might be instructive. When I graduated from college, I was perplexed about a future career, but I enrolled in law school with the intention of becoming a lawyer as my father had been. I had concentrated in English in college, however, and so I also took the Graduate Record Examinations for possible entrance into graduate school in English. As I was taking them, I encountered a passage to identify, which I have always thought (I cannot remember on what clue) came from Edwin Arlington Robinson's *Tristram,* and was about birds and sunlight and water. Perhaps it was even this passage:

> . . . waves and foam
> And white birds everywhere, flying, and flying;
> Alone, with her white face and her gray eyes,
> She watched them there till even her thoughts were white,
> And there was nothing alive but white birds flying,
> Flying, and always flying, and still flying,
> And the white sunlight flashing on the sea.

In any event, whether it was this passage or some other, possibly even from some other poem, I was so powerfully affected that I left the examination room in a kind of intoxication. I had experienced a feeling of completeness and certainty, one so strong indeed that I not only thought about it for weeks afterward but even, and almost as a matter of course, withdrew from law school and enrolled in graduate school at least in part in order to try to be closer to the transcendent meaning I had experienced.

A still later experience of transcendent meaning occurred when I was studying in Europe. A girl had given me a ticket to a performance of Bach's *Weihnachtsoratorium*, which was to take place just before Christmas in a church where Melanchthon had preached. When the piece began, with kettle drums pounding and clarino trumpets soaring, I had an almost physical sensation of being hurled from my chair against one of the pillars of the church. More significantly, I was in a state of intoxication for weeks after the event, and whenever even months later I happened to think of the moment I felt an upsurge of joy.

The last time such transcendent meaning revealed itself to me was when I was in my early thirties. I had come home to visit my mother. As such occasions were rather uneventful for me, I was accustomed to spending a certain amount of time reading cheap novels, and in this instance I had left her apartment and was walking down to the corner drugstore to borrow a mystery story from the lending library there. It was a spring afternoon, evening coming on, the air wonderfully light and cool, the leaves rustling, the sunlight golden through them. Suddenly I was overwhelmed by the fullness of being. All the sense of struggle in life ceased, all the sense of future, of something ever more about to be. All that needed to be, all that could be, was present to me.

I can hardly expect others to share in such intensely personal memories, especially when the ineffable feelings they entailed are no longer available even to me. But perhaps by adding some further examples from the public domain of culture to those from the certainty of my private experience, I can at least begin to persuade the skeptic of the existence, even if not the essence, of the truths I am attempting to signalize.

The text I shall set out from is Dorothy Wordsworth's Alfoxden Journal. It begins with the mysterious intensity that characterizes it throughout:

Alfoxden, 20th January 1798. The green paths down the hillsides are channels for streams. The young wheat is streaked by silver lines of water running between the ridges, the sheep are gathered together on the slopes. After the wet dark days, the

country seems more populous. It peoples itself in the sun-
beams. The garden, mimic of spring, is gay with flowers. The
purple-starred hepatica spreads itself in the sun, and the clus-
tering snow-drops put forth their white heads, at first upright,
ribbed with green, and like a rosebud; when completely opened,
hanging their heads downwards, but slowly lengthening their
slender stems. The slanting woods of an unvarying brown,
showing the light through the thin net-work of their upper
boughs. Upon the highest ridge of that round hill, covered with
planted oaks, the shafts of the trees show in the light like the
columns of a ruin.

The language is extraordinary; it seems to be more that of a poem
than of a simple journal record. Indeed, if set off in a manner of free
verse, it would constitute a poem of distinct power:

> The green paths down the hillsides are channels for streams.
> The young wheat is streaked by silver lines
> Of water running between the ridges.
> The sheep are gathered together on the slopes.
> After the wet dark days, the country seems more populous.
> It peoples itself in the sunbeams.
> The garden, mimic of spring, is gay with flowers.
> The purple-starred hepatica spreads itself in the sun,
> And the clustering snow-drops put forth their white heads. . . .

There is a paradoxical relationship between the extreme intensity
of the language and the absence of happening, or rather the absence
of anything conventionally considered an important event. Nothing
much takes place; things simply are. But their areness, impregnated
by the language, seems apocalyptic. Wonder invests the simple apprehension, "The sheep are gathered together on the slopes." The
date, 20th January 1798, is peculiarly urgent; it seems to indicate an
attempt to fix this wonder before it can dissipate. It is, as it were, an
aperture, a narrow window, through which being itself is glimpsed.

There is a pervasive pregnancy in Dorothy Wordsworth's entries.
Commonplace of happening is transformed to apocalyptic presence
by the intensity of the language. To be sure, there is something of

that in Somerset itself, where the sense and sound of the unseen Western sea behind a peaceful, cow-grazed hillside lends an uncanny expectancy to what elsewhere would be merely bucolic—"So might I, standing on this pleasant lea, / Have glimpses that would make me less forlorn; / Have sight of Proteus rising from the sea." But Dorothy Wordsworth's intensity augments that inherent situation. Little of importance actually occurs, but the passages are invested with the sense that something of apocalyptic finality is happening:

> January 26th. Walked upon the hill-tops; followed the sheep tracks till we overlooked the larger coombe. Sat in the sunshine. The distant sheep-bells, the sound of the stream; the woodman winding along the half-marked road with his laden pony; locks of wool still spangled with dewdrops; the blue-grey sea, shaded with immense masses of cloud, not streaked; the sheep glittering in the sunshine. Returned through the wood. The trees skirting the wood, being exposed more directly to the action of the sea breeze, stripped of the network of their upper boughs, which are stiff and erect, like black skeletons; the ground strewed with the red berries of the holly. Set forward before two o'clock. Returned a little after four.

The sense of urgent meaning is conveyed even when such meticulous observation cannot be achieved:

> 1st March. We rose early. A thick fog obscured the distant prospect entirely, but the shapes of the nearer trees and dome of the wood dimly seen and dilated. It cleared away between ten and eleven. The shapes of the mist, slowly moving along, exquisitely beautiful; passing over the sheep they almost seemed to have more of life than those quiet creatures. The unseen birds singing in the mist.

"The unseen birds singing in the mist" in this apprehension partakes of the same wonder as the simple "Sat in the sunshine" of the previous grasping of being.

What Dorothy Wordsworth continually proffers is the third kind of meaning. The fullness of her evocation is the pregnancy of being.

The sense of supreme importance is not meaning by equivalence; it is meaning transcendent:

> 3rd February. A mild morning, the windows open at breakfast, the redbreasts singing in the garden. Walked with Coleridge over the hills. The sea at first obscured by vapour; that vapour afterwards slid in one mighty mass along the sea-shore; the islands and one point of land clear beyond it. The distant country (which was purple in the clear dull air), overhung by straggling clouds that sailed over it. . . . I never saw such a union of earth, sky and sea. The clouds beneath our feet spread themselves to the water, and the clouds of the sky almost joined them. Gathered sticks in the wood; a perfect stillness. The redbreasts sang upon the leafless boughs. Of a great number of sheep in the field, only one standing. Returned to dinner at five o'clock. The moonlight still and warm as a summer's night at nine o'clock.

The simple specifications "Gathered sticks in the wood" or "The redbreasts sang upon the leafless boughs" indicate the third kind of meaning, but they are not translatable. That is to say, the words can be translated but their meaning cannot.

Dorothy Wordsworth is especially germane to the conception of the third kind of meaning, because there is no hint of mysticism in what she says, as there was none in my own experience of that kind of meaning. Doubtless all mystic experience is transcendent meaning, but it does not follow that all transcendent meaning is mystical. Indeed, if the reality of transcendent meaning is to function in a general theory of culture, it must be separated from mysticism.

Actually, one is led to suspect that much of what is loosely called "mysticism" is simply a hasty and superficial recognition (and dismissal) of the experience of the third kind of meaning. When Coleridge in 1818 termed Blake "a mystic emphatically," he spoke in the terms that dominated Blake criticism for more than a century. Even Foster Damon's important study of 1924 considered Blake "a mystic." All that has changed in the last half-century, however, perhaps beginning with the studies by Percival and by Schorer, and today critics who think Blake a mystic are few and unheeded. Though personally a witness to the third kind of meaning, he was neither mystical nor mad, but rather a participant in a well-defined tradition, and quite content to indulge in a certain kind of rhetorical play that catered to the eagerness of his hearers to speak of mysticism (or madness, as the case might be).

The same might be said for such an important figure in Blake's antecedence as Jakob Boehme. Called the "greatest of all mystics" by Berdyaev, the "most comprehensive, richest and most various of all mystics" by Friedrich Schlegel, Boehme was, one must on the contrary insist, very probably not a mystic at all. He functioned as a well-informed participant in subterranean Hermetic and Cabalistic learning, a learning shared by many of his friends and compeers and mediated by an intense prior lineage in German thought. What is often brought forward as testimony to his mysticism, the story told by his early biographer, Franckenberg, of his penetrating into the "innermost ground or center" of things by a glance cast upon "a bright pewter dish," seems to me not only not mystical, but in truth very much like my own experience of looking at the bushes in the twilight.

Be that as it may, if one still demands an example of transcendent meaning that could be termed "mystical" (I defer to that specific description as offered by David Ferry), one might be content with Ferry's citation of that passage in William Wordsworth's "Tintern Abbey" where reference is made to

> . . . that blessed mood,
> In which the burthen of the mystery
> In which the heavy and the weary weight
> Of all this unintelligible world,
> Is lightened:—that serene and blessed mood,
> In which the affections gently lead us on,—
> Until, the breath of this corporeal frame
> And even the motion of our human blood
> Almost suspended we are laid asleep
> In body, and become a living soul:

> While with an eye made quiet by the power
> Of harmony, and the deep power of joy,
> We see into the life of things.

Wordsworth signalizes the rarefied nature of the experience by conceding, in the next line, that what he has described might be "but a vain belief"; and to the skeptic, that possibility is always open for any mystic experience.

But what Dorothy Wordsworth apprehends is not mystic. Transcendent meaning that is not mystic, again, is what Dostoevsky points to in *The Brothers Karamazov* in the chapter about Father Zossima's brother:

> "Don't cry mother," he would answer, "life is paradise, and we are all in paradise, but we won't see it, if we would we should have heaven on earth the next day."

The wonder is insistent:

> "You'll live many days yet," the doctor would answer, "and months and years too."
>
> "Months and years!" he would exclaim. "Why reckon the days? One day is enough for a man to know all happiness. My dear ones, why do we quarrel, try to outshine each other and keep grudges against each other? Let's go straight into the garden, walk and play there, love, appreciate, and kiss each other, and glorify life."
>
> "Your son cannot last long," the doctor told my mother, as she accompanied him to the door. "The disease is affecting his brain."

The doctor's comment serves to set off the ordinary world of equivalent meanings from those meanings apprehended by the brother: "'Yes,' he said, 'there was such a glory of God all about me; birds, trees, meadows, sky, only I lived in shame and did not notice the beauty and glory.'"

Transcendent but not mystic meaning is also pointed to by the supreme passage in *King Lear:*

No, no, no, no! Come, let's away to prison;
We two alone will sing like birds i' th' cage:
When thou dost ask me blessing, I'll kneel down,
And ask of thee forgiveness: so we'll live,
And pray, and sing, and tell old tales, and laugh
At gilded butterflies, and hear poor rogues
Talk of court news; and we'll talk with them too,
Who loses and who wins; who's in, who's out;
And take upon's the mystery of things,
As if we were God's spies: and we'll wear out,
In a wall'd prison, packs and sects of great ones
That ebb and flow by th' moon.

The famous passage has many peripheral meanings that are meanings by equivalence, and critics and scholars can discourse richly of
its rhetorical and imagistic configurations, as well as of the way the
language takes up motifs prepared earlier in the words and situation
of the play. But its essential meaning is not meaning by equivalence
but transcendent meaning. To "laugh at gilded butterflies" is an action of the same order of meaning as Dorothy Wordsworth's "We sat
in the sunshine." "We'll live, / And pray, and sing, and tell old tales"
is a statement of the same order of meaning as Dostoevsky's "Let's
go straight into the garden, walk and play there, love, appreciate,
and kiss each other, and glorify life."

Of the same order of meaning, too, though in a matrix and mode
entirely different, is a passage near the conclusion of Jane Austen's
Persuasion:

Soon words enough had passed between them to decide their
direction towards the comparatively quiet and retired gravel-
walk, where the power of conversation would make the present
hour a blessing indeed; and prepare for it all the immortality
which the happiest recollections of their own future lives could
bestow. There they exchanged once again those feelings and
those promises which had once before seemed to secure every
thing, but which had been followed by so many, many years of
division and estrangement. There they returned again into the

past, more exquisitely happy, perhaps, in their re-union, than when it had been first projected; more tender, more tried, more fixed in a knowledge of each other's character, truth, and attachment; more equal to act, more justified in acting. And there, as they slowly paced the gradual ascent, heedless of every group around them, seeing neither sauntering politicians, bustling house-keepers, flirting girls, nor nursery-maids and children, they could indulge in those retrospections and acknowledgments, and especially in those explanations of what directly preceded the present moment, which were so poignant and so ceaseless in interest. All the little variations of the last week were gone through; and of yesterday and to-day there could scarcely be an end.

Anne Elliot and Captain Wentworth, like Cordelia and Lear, are "more exquisitely happy . . . in their re-union" than in their earlier bond, "more tender, more tried, more fixed in a knowledge of each other's character, truth, and attachment." Like Cordelia and Lear— "we two alone"—they are in their mutual happiness raised above the world of the striving many: the "poor rogues" who "Talk of court news . . . / Who loses and who wins; who's in, who's out," are coordinate with the "sauntering politicians, bustling house-keepers, flirting girls . . . nursery-maids and children" to whom the lovers, in their new being, are heedless and superior. "When thou dost ask me blessing, I'll kneel down, / And ask of thee forgiveness" is a statement of backward-looking mutuality much like the exchange "once again" of "those feelings and those promises which had once before seemed to secure every thing." Anne and Captain Wentworth "returned again into the past," engaged in "retrospections"; Lear and Cordelia will "tell old tales."

Like the passage from *King Lear,* the passage from *Persuasion* involves meanings by equivalence; but like that passage, too, it bears its essential meaning, its melody of the soul, as a transcendent entity that cannot be translated but only experienced. Perhaps the closest analogy in music to the special structure of grace and certainty, the confident and inevitable happiness, of Jane Austen's vision here, is that offered by the coda in the last movement of Haydn's Symphony No. 98 in B.

If transcendent meaning is not experienced by everyone, it obviously is not necessary to human life; yet it is the pursuit of transcendent meaning that sets culture in motion. How such meaning can at once be superior to primary meaning and at the same time secondary to it—superior to meaning by equivalence and at the same time not necessary—may be grasped by analogy. When I was a child, I was noteworthy for the acuteness of my eyesight. My vision was not only extraordinarily keen, but my perceptions of color and depth were also remarkable, so much so that eye examinations invariably occasioned murmurs and comment from those doing the testing. My parents, however, had poor vision and could not function effectively without glasses. I used to wonder what they saw, and I would often squint my eyes to try to participate in the half-world I thought they must inhabit. Now that I too cannot read without glasses, I accept this half-world as the norm. The necessary thing is that I see, although much less well than I once did. Mutatis mutandis, the same relation obtains between transcendent meaning and primary meaning; the former is an exceptionally acute form of primary meaning, where one clearly and unmistakably sees things that are not seen by the other meaning. The other meaning is universal; transcendent meaning is vouchsafed only to the few.

Yet in the cumulative testimony of cultural history, transcendent meaning is everywhere to be encountered. It is at the heart of mankind's preoccupation with the statements of lyric poetry, the core of which is the effort to regain such meaning; it is at the heart of the enormous impact the Christian religion has had in world history, an impact of which the search for the lost memory of transcendent meaning is the motive component; it is the reason for museums, concerts, and research libraries; it is at the foundation of all the structures of politeness, benign social custom, and morality. As the very few examples just brought forward from differing realms of culture suggest, it is the final goal of great artists in all the arts. Indeed, though Marxist theory considers the whole of culture to be a superstructure secondary to and derived from the economic infrastructure, this description can apply only to those meanings by equivalence in which the business of culture is transacted. The third kind of meaning that sets culture in motion lies outside both infrastructure and superstructure; and it is significant that though the theory of superstructures can account for culture once culture is given, it cannot say why culture should exist in the first place.

The sum of the foregoing observations about the relationship of the third kind of meaning to the strivings of culture comprises a corollary, as it were, to Wittgenstein's conclusion: "Whereof one cannot speak, thereof one must be silent" ("Wovon man nicht sprechen kann, darüber muss man schweigen"). The third kind of meaning is ineffable, a "wovon" that cannot be uttered. It follows that it is necessary to be silent about what it is. But the cumulative witness of culture is that the *attempt* to grasp the "wovon," as contrasted to the actual grasping of it, has generated a continuing antithesis of silence. "Das Wort erstirbt schon in der Feder," laments Faust—"The word dies when we take up the pen"—and yet the pen is forever taken up again. For Keats, an elusive and unattained "vast idea" which "ever rolls" before him was the "end and aim of poetry."

The mighty hum of aspiration never stops: typewriters are chattering and word processors whispering, ceaselessly, violins are being tuned, sculptures cast, paints mixed, rhyming dictionaries opened, cadences tested, stories concocted, all toward the "wovon" of which humans cannot speak but about which they cannot remain silent. And the periodic eruption of this constant preluding roar into the language of symphonies, poems, and other cultural endeavor is an expression of the need to reclaim something once experienced, momentarily but intensely. Though many people participate as a predictable consequence of the sociological structure of art—many become musicians, for instance, merely because musical activity exists as an established enterprise of society—the movers of culture, the few and the great, are forever attempting to reclaim something. "The end then of learning," says one of those few and great, speaking of the whole enormous and unending business, "is to repair the ruins of our first parents. . . ." Or bring to the mind's eye the paintings and drawings of Picasso's last decade. "The belief is at least tenable," notes Paul Fry in *The Reach of Criticism*, "that written texts are not to be understood most radically as modes of production but as modes of substitution, as ways of recovering the experience of being."

Even if it is the existence of transcendent meaning that sets culture in motion, that meaning stands itself outside of culture. I remember reading some years ago of the discovery of a paleolithic burial site that the paleontologists were able to date as stemming from thirty thousand years ago, a time prior to any known culture whatever; poignantly, the site was lined by the traces of flowers that were an evanescent reminder of human grief. Death is simply a fact; its connection with grief, and of grief with the signification of flowers, points to transcendent meaning.

Though paradoxically not part either of the foundation or of the business of culture, transcendent meaning is sighted repeatedly in the cultural expression of the last two and a half millennia. For a single additional instance, in Dostoevsky's *The Idiot*, Prince Myshkin muses about certain states when "there seemed at moments a flash of light in his brain, and with extraordinary impetus all his vital forces suddenly began working at their highest tension." It is characteristic of the third kind of meaning that "the sense of life, the consciousness of self, were multiplied ten times at these moments. . . . His mind and his heart were flooded with extraordinary light; all his uneasiness, all his doubts, all his anxieties were relieved at once; they were all merged in a lofty calm, full of serene, harmonious joy and hope." Wondering whether such moments are diseased in their abnormal intensity (and Myshkin's meditation is in fact depicted as the prelude to an epileptic seizure, which one surmises, as with the doctor's comment about Father Zossima's brother, that "the disease is affecting his brain," is a device by which Dostoevsky seeks to protect his most personal experience from ridicule), Myshkin concludes that it can hardly matter, so long as the moment "gives a feeling, unknown and undivined till then, of completeness, of proportion, of reconciliation." He insists on the clarity and certainty of the experience: "It was not as though he saw abnormal and unreal visions of some sort at the moment, as from hashish, opium, or wine, destroying the reason and distorting the soul." On the contrary, as has been urged throughout this discussion, "these moments were only an extraordinary quickening of self-consciousness" and at the same time bearers "of the direct sensation of existence in the most intense degree." Significantly, an enormous value is placed on such experience, for Dostoevsky goes on to say that Myshkin "actually had said to himself at that second, that, for the infinite happiness he had felt in it, that second really might well be worth the whole of life."

Of special importance for the viability of shapes of culture as replacements for forms is that such moments of transcendent meaning are characterized, as Dostoevsky urges and as I experienced, by "completeness." The ramified and extended connections of knowledge and its cultural forms are irrelevant to such fullness. Thus, though strictly speaking only disconnected parts of human awareness, as shapes are disconnected parts of knowledge, such moments by their completeness energize as well as fit the shapes, and can validate them for cultural function independently of the forms of knowledge. Where completeness reigns, other knowledge is not necessary.

These moments of meaning generate the endeavors of culture, even though they stand outside those endeavors. Recently I chanced to see a documentary on the public television channel detailing the process of competition for the Van Cliburn Prize in piano performance. It was a fascinating story: several dozen youthful contestants coming together for three weeks of competition mixed with social conviviality. Intensity was palpable. The documentary personally acquainted the viewer with the aspiring performers, as it were, and followed them through all the stages of the competition. Remarkably, none of their work, none of their technique, had value of itself. Some of the judges attempted to explain what they were listening for: not merely to hear the notes played accurately but to hear them played in a way that brought tears to the eyes—in a way, that is, that stood outside all this endeavor. One of the judges, the pianist Malcolm Frager, said early on that one of the performers, unnamed, stood above the others and was already an artist. Yet all the performers were technically proficient. Indeed, the pianist who won, José Feghali, was perhaps not quite so proficient as the runner-up. But by the poignance of his playing he revealed himself to be reaching for the third kind of meaning, the "wovon" that could not be expressed but hovered just beyond the music as an articulation of sound. The notes were the same for any pianist; only the pianist who was able to play them toward their transcendence could hope to conquer the judges.

Interestingly, and symptomatic of the elusiveness of the third kind of meaning, a later review of Feghali's playing at Carnegie Hall, in the *New York Times* of October 21, 1985, precisely complained of the absence of poignance: "Mr. Feghali seemed to me a skilled orator without a topic. . . . Haydn's E Flat Sonata . . . was probably intended as a warm-up piece but it was in truth a damning litmus test of this pianist's stage of development. The Adagio's rising dotted rhythms had none of Haydn's plaintiveness. . . ." And the reviewer concluded that the pianist at the present moment "is neither intellectually nor spiritually equipped for the spotlight into which he has been cast."

But intensities of meaning, either those found lacking here or those of Prince Myshkin's "direct sensation of existence in the most intense degree," do not comprehensibly constitute the edifice of culture. The foundation is made up of primary meanings; the building, as urged above, is almost wholly erected in terms of meaning by equivalence, which are an endless series of transformations that actually evade and defer the question of meaning. In this sense it can be said that almost the whole of the visible structure of culture is a form of translation.

This larger kind of translation, that is, meaning by equivalence, includes within it those translations from one language to another that elicit the use of the word in ordinary discourse. Thus, for instance, Werner Jaeger notes in his *Early Christianity and Greek Paideia:*

One can understand the historical development of the Christian religion during the first centuries as a process of continuous "translation" of its sources, aimed at giving the world an ever more accurate understanding and realization of their content. The process began when the first evangelists, going back to the earliest extant oral or written reports of the sayings and doings of Jesus, translated them from the original Aramaic into Greek and arranged them in their present form. A further step was taken when a writer like Luke, with his better education in Greek, found those early translations defective in language and presentation of the material and tried to adjust their form to his own higher standards. But translation in that literal sense was only a first attempt to get at the meaning of the original words. . . . The interpretative process was thereby automatically transferred to a higher level, and it took great minds to approach this formidable task.

The tenor of this quotation from Jaeger marks a turning in what I am trying to say. The argument for the next several pages and more will follow the convolutions of a single topic: literary translation. The examples brought forward, as indeed the topic itself, may seem digressive, or at least less serious than the argument till now; but the discussion as a whole constitutes a prologue to the book's special interpretation of the nature and meaning of cultural activity. In Jaeger's passage we see the enunciation of a double truth: translation from one language to another is merely a special focus of a larger transfer of meaning; but by the same token the primary problem of such transfers is always in some sense an attempt to lift the curse of Babel, which is not simply the fragmentation of language but the fragmentation of the forms of knowing. Indeed, George Steiner, in his *After Babel,* specifically addresses the problems of translations between language as a special instance of the general structure of civilized understanding. "A human being," says Steiner, "performs an act of translation, in the full sense of the word, when receiving a speech-message from any other human being."

Translation, however, is not a monolithic activity; rather it reveals itself in at least three distinct and different structures, all of them important, and each accreting around a different principle that defines its nature, use, and limitation. These three principles that underlie all translational activity are *attenuation, dispersal,* and *impedance.* It will be necessary to investigate two of the three in order to realize the full range of relationship that occurs between meanings by experience and those displacements into meanings by equivalence that constitute culture, and that validate shapes of culture as replacements for forms of culture.

What we most commonly and directly think of as translation, that is, the simple movement of a text from one spoken and written language of a given ethnographic or geographic group to another, is a topic of increasing importance in modern intellectual life. The ease of travel by jet planes, the visual proximity of television images transmitted by satellite, the general contraction of the varieties and possibilities of experience, have all combined to render the crossing of the barriers of language more urgent than ever before. A sign of the times is the R. R. Bowker Company's publication of a volume called *Translation and Translators: An International Directory and Guide,* which, as the advertisement announces, "provides information on the translating profession previously available only in parts, and never before assembled in one place." The advertisement continues: "After centuries of being a neglected and underpaid profession, translation is at last coming into its own."

To be sure, translation has actually been important for a long time. Almost all poets, even those who do not know comparative languages very well, hone their poetic skills, so to speak, by exercises in translation. Shelley, for instance, could hardly claim to know German at all, but he embarked on a translation of Goethe's *Faust.* He knew Greek very well, and translated and imitated numerous ancient texts, his translation of Plato's *Symposium* being especially noteworthy. Translation from Latin, Italian, Spanish, and French was also part of his agenda. Again, at random, one can point in contemporary times to Richard Wilbur's translations of Molière, Marianne Moore's of La Fontaine, or James Wright's of Trakl from German and Neruda from Spanish. One may think back to Chaucer's translation of Boethius from Latin and Jean de Meun from French. Or one can simply bring to mind F. O. Matthiessen's dissertation *Translation, an Elizabethan Art.* The growth of culture has always been a straining against the barriers of language. As Rousseau said of Émile's education, "If he has the least glimmering of taste in poetry, how eagerly will he study the languages of the poets, Greek, Latin, and Italian!"

The learning of alternative languages is an attempt to obviate the attenuations of translation. One of Hegel's arguments for the continued study of the classical languages was precisely this contention:

> . . . content can be approximately given us by translations, but not the form, not the ethereal soul. Translations are like artificial roses that may resemble real ones in shape, color, and perhaps even scent, but that cannot attain their loveliness, delicacy and softness of life. . . . The language is the musical element, the element of intimacy that fades away in the translation; it is the fine fragrance that makes possible the reader's sympathetic enjoyment of the ancient work. . . .

Again, Mommsen, in 1874, told his students that "he who leaves the university with a thorough knowledge of the Latin, Greek and German languages . . . is prepared to be a historian"; and he urged that such preparation was better than that provided by historiography itself:

> I confess, Gentlemen, if I find from your papers that you are students of history I shall be all anxiety. . . . It might mean that you think . . . you will take refuge in history from all the difficulties of rigorous philology and rest content with a painstaking investigation of sources and a study of the method of writing history. Where this is the case, nemesis will not be long delayed. . . . The lack of genuine preparation will bring vengeance upon you. . . .

And yet the learning of languages in order to forestall translation is a homeopathic remedy at best, for to acquire a language other than one learned as a native speaker is, so to speak, to tunnel across from one basement to another, rather than using the translational bridge on the top floor. The second language will itself be a form of translation. Rousseau maintains that it is possible for a child to "learn to speak only one language. I am told, however, that he speaks several. I deny it. I have seen these little prodigies who believed that they spoke five or six languages. I have heard them speak German in Latin terms, in French terms, in Italian terms successively. They did in truth make use of five or six lexicons. But they always spoke only German."

At all events, and notwithstanding historically entrenched earlier commitments to various forms of language acquirement and translation, the importance of simple translation is unmistakably accelerating today, as economic and social proximities reinforce intellectual traditions. Operating instructions for goods in any modern shop are now characteristically presented in several languages. It is hardly surprising, therefore, that along with the traditional commitment of poets to translation, almost every intellectual, the scientist no less than the humanist, has some awareness of translational theory today, and most have, or feel they ought to have, a position with regard to so pressing a topic. When Reuben Brower, in 1959, or William Arrowsmith in 1964 and again in 1971, published anthologies of modern opinion on the subject, their volumes were thronged with contributions from thinkers of diverse backgrounds and heterogeneous attainments. But these volumes are merely tips of the theoretical iceberg.

Despite much attention in many languages, however, the theory of translation remains in a rudimentary state. Indeed, through translation itself is an omnipresent activity, the theory of translation can hardly be said to exist. With regard to poems, as we all know, there are fairly good and fairly poor translations, but little understanding of how either comes about; and as to theory itself, the best known version (is it Frost's?) is the most cynical—I mean the *mot* urging that poetry can be defined as what gets left out when a poem is translated. Both the appropriateness of the cynicism and the radical paradoxicality of the situation with regard to translational activity are focused by Shelley, who despite his commitment to such activity, nevertheless denounces "the vanity of translation": "It were as wise to cast a violet into a crucible that you might discover the formal principle of its colour and odour, as seek to transfuse from one language into another the creations of a poet. The plant must spring again from its seed, or it will bear no flower—and this is the burthen of the curse of Babel." To the truth of that observation all must agree. Cervantes, to cite a single confirmatory example, refers in the sixth chapter of the first book of *Don Quixote* to a translation of Ariosto, who has "been brought to Spain and turned into a Castilian, thereby robbing him of much of his native charm. This is what happens to all who translate books of verse into another tongue, for in spite of all the trouble they take and the skill they may display, they will never reach the level of the original."

Even the best translation is only an approximation, and few would attempt to contravene the opinion of Robert Martin Adams, in his volume on literary translation called *Proteus, His Lies, His Truth:*

> That, after all, is the point: translation, which can be an exhilaration for the translator, and an amusement for the critical student, is a snare and a delusion for the man who takes it at face value. Though convenient and sometimes indispensable as a crutch, it is grossly inadequate as a wooden leg. Because it is always a compromise, and great art is rarely a compromise, the odds are always against it.
>
> If a formula for literature is a contradiction in terms, so (doubly) is the idea of a ratio for the success of literary translation. At best, translation is a set of desperate gambles, and like all gambles recommended only for those who have secure investments elsewhere. . . . Almost always, those people enjoy translations most who need them least; this is a regrettable instance of the old rule governing literary interpretation, that whosoever hath, to him shall be given. It is sad but true that reading a translation by itself is like looking at a landscape with one eye and it half-shut.

After observing that "translations as means of access to an original" are merely "better and worse instances of a secondhand experience," Adams concludes his book with a whimper: "When the blind lead the blind, there's a very good chance they will both fall into the ditch; but when the ditches are full of vocal unfortunates, a man may very well guide himself a little way onward through the darkness by the noise of their clamor."

To the question of why, with so little light, he dares take on the topic of translation, Adams answers with disarming humility that "impossible subjects may be well worth discussing. . . . However far it falls short of the genuinely 'adequate,' such a discussion may aspire to widen a few horizons and organize a few standing prejudices"; and, walking softly and carrying no stick at all, he pleads in a noticeably conciliatory tone that "an effort to rationalize so chaotic a subject, if only by a degree or two, can hardly be amiss."

Humility may hardly seem a satisfactory substitute for enlightenment, but Adams is not the only commentator who becomes meek and self-deprecating when confronted by the elusiveness of translation. Consider, for a single additional instance, the rueful confession of Roger Shattuck about his labors as a translator of Apollinaire: "my principal credential as a translator is that of having published several of the most horrendous bloomers in translation in this century, one of them cited (namelessly) by Justin O'Brien in [an] article on translations from the French."

This is all no doubt embarrassing enough, but mistakes in translation are not the real problem; rather it is the elusiveness of textual essence even when no mistakes are present. No one would argue that Gilbert Murray was deficient in his knowledge of ancient Greek, and yet no one, I think, can fail to concede that T. S. Eliot was entirely in the right in his attacks on the satisfactoriness of Murray's translations of Euripides.

Again, though from Chapman and Pope to Lattimore and Fitzgerald distinguished effort has gone into the translation of Homer, unfortunately, to paraphrase Bentley's celebrated comment to Pope, "it's not Homer"—not exactly, that is, even though Matthew Arnold tries to tell us how one ought to go about it. Oscar Wilde thinks well of William Morris's translation of *The Odyssey* and clearly is trying to be gracious:

> Of all our modern poets, Mr. William Morris is the one best qualified by nature and by art to translate for us the marvellous epic of the wanderings of Odysseus. . . . Master as he is of decorative and descriptive verse, he has all the Greek's joy in the visible aspect of things, all the Greek's sense of delicate and delightful detail, all the Greek's pleasure in beautiful textures and exquisite materials and imaginative designs; nor can any one have a keener sympathy with the Homeric admiration for the workers and the craftsmen in the various arts, from the stainers in white ivory and the embroiderers in purple and gold, to the weaver sitting by the loom and the dyer dipping in the

vat, the chaser of shield and helmet, the carver of wood or stone. And to all this is added the true temper of high romance, the power to make the past as real to us as the present, the subtle instinct to discern passion, the swift impulse to portray life.

Accordingly, Wilde writes that "it is not extravagant to say that of all our English translations this is the most perfect and the most satisfying." "Here we have a true work of art, a rendering not merely of language into language, but of poetry into poetry."

But then qualifications begin to creep in. The "translation may seem to some more Norse than Greek, and, perhaps at times, more boisterous than beautiful." "It may be admitted at once that, here and there, Mr. Morris has missed something of the marvellous dignity of the Homeric verse, and that, in his desire for rushing and ringing metre, he has occasionally sacrificed majesty to movement." When in a second article Wilde reviewed the second part of Morris's translation the same ambivalence of praise and reservation obtained:

> It is not too much to say that Mr. Morris's version will always be a true classic amongst our classical translations. It is not, of course, flawless. In our notice of the first volume we ventured to say that Mr. Morris was sometimes far more Norse than Greek, nor does the volume that now lies before us make us alter that opinion. The particular metre, also, selected by Mr. Morris, although admirably adapted to express "the strong-winged music of Homer," as far as its flow and freedom are concerned, misses something of its dignity and calm. Here, it must be admitted, we feel a distinct loss, for there is in Homer not a little of Milton's lofty manner, and if swiftness be an essential of the Greek hexameter, stateliness is one of its distinguishing qualities in Homer's hands.

If translation is at best an approximation, it is also probably true that the less literary merit possessed by a work in its original tongue, the better the translation is enabled to become. Directions to the toilet are eloquent in all languages. Those translations of operating instructions in four languages, noted above, for electrical equipment made in Europe or Japan, are superb in their exactitude. Translations of business letters are better than translations of novels. Translations of novels are better than translations of long poems. Translations of long poems tend to be better than translations of short poems. The finest functioning translators may well be such full-time professional prose specialists as Ralph Manheim rather than any of the numerous and sensitive poet-translators.

Manheim perhaps knows his parallel languages better than do most of the poet-translators, but that is not the real ground of his superiority. It is rather that the poet-translators are, as it were, attempting to shovel smoke. Or, to vary the metaphor, the poet attempting to translate a fellow poet from a foreign tongue is like a master pastry chef who thinks to squeeze onto the pastry sheet one of those fluffy solid doughnuts called in Germany "ein Berliner." He brings his mastery to bear, but instead of a solid doughnut, out comes one with a hole in the center. He cleans his equipment, remixes his batter, and proceeds to squeeze again. Once again out comes a doughnut, but again and evermore one with a hole in the center.

This hole in the center, the void where the poetry was, is what poet-translators seek to fill. But it is the eternal hole in the center that attenuates all attempts to reach the theoretically apodictic. Instead of theory, there are in translation merely practical facts and problems of linguistic equivalence on the one hand, and cascading paradox on the other. Paradox, I mean, of the double sort pointed out by Kenneth Rexroth:

> Sympathy can carry you very far if you have talent to go with it. Hart Crane never learned to speak French and at the time he wrote his triptych poems *Voyages* he could not read it at all. His only informant was Allen Tate, a doubtful guide at best in this field, and his image of Rimbaud was an absurd inflation of the absurd Rimbaud myth. Yet *Voyages* is by far the best transmission of Rimbaud into English that exists—the purest distillation of the boyish hallucinations of *Bateau Ivre*.

Sympathy, or at least projection, can carry you too far. All sensible men to whom English is native are distressed by the French enthusiasm for M. Poe, the author of *Jamais Plus*. Nobody in France seems to be able to learn, ever, that his verse is dreadful doggerel and his ratiocinative fiction absurd and his aesthetics the standard lucubrations. . . . The reason is, of course, that the French translate their whole culture into Poe before they even start to read him.

A more intricate cascade of paradox, in a less subjective context, can be realized if we approach Dryden, who is a central figure in both the practice of translation and its theoretical problems. As William Frost says, in his *Dryden and the Art of Translation:*

As a poet . . . Dryden devoted most of his energies to translation. . . . For every line of original nondramatic poetry he wrote two lines of translation from a foreign poet.

Far from being apprentice work, Dryden's translations were, for his contemporaries at least, the climax of his poetic career. More than nine-tenths of them—measured, again, in sheer number of lines—were published during the last decade of his life, and these include his most mature and impressive work in the genre: the Juvenal and Persius in 1692; the complete Virgil in 1697; and the selections from Chaucer, Ovid, Boccaccio, and Homer in the *Fables* volume of 1700, the year of his death. The Virgil, which appears to have consumed the labor of about four years, is itself as long as all Dryden's original poetry put together. Of his best translations, only the bits of Horace and Lucretius in the Sylvae anthology of 1685 were published before 1690; all the rest fall within the final decade.

Despite this impressive listing of Dryden's efforts at translation, however, Frost shortly afterward begins a discussion of the theory of translation under the subheading "The Theoretical Impossibility of Translation," and continues with another section called "False Expectations as to Translation." He concludes that "the translator is always confronting a kind of chaos. . . . He must therefore create a new artifact out of the rubble of dictionary meanings extracted from the old poem." And he posits two criteria for the success of a verse translation: "I think it can be fairly well demonstrated that a poem which purports to translate a foreign poem will, if successful, constitute both (1) a new English poem of intrinsic interest and (2) an interpretation of the original on which it was based. . . ." But this retreat into a theory of translation as interpretation runs head-on into the theoretical prescription of Dryden's contemporary the Earl of Roscommon, who in his *Essay on Translated Verse* of 1684 writes as follows:

> Then seek a Poet who your way do's bend,
> And chuse an Author as you chuse a Friend:
> United by the Sympathetick Bond,
> You grow Familiar, Intimate, and Fond;
> Your thoughts, your Words, your Sides, your Souls agree,
> No longer his Interpreter, but He.

Frost's notion of translation as "an interpretation of the original on which it was based" is thus locked in unresolved paradox with Roscommon's notion that the ideal translator become "No longer his Interpreter, but He." Nor is the paradox formed simply by juxtaposing Frost's twentieth-century view against Roscommon's seventeenth-century one. If we substitute for Frost's view the opinion of Dryden himself, according to which translation is actually paraphrase, "where the author is kept in view by the translator, so as never to be lost, but his words are not so strictly followed as his sense; and that too is admitted to be amplified, but not altered," then the paradox still stands.

Indeed, the topic ramifies almost endlessly, and paradox accompanies it through all its windings. Thus, despite Dryden's great commitment to both the theory and practice of translation, Wordsworth can cruelly judge that

> Dryden had neither a tender heart nor a lofty sense of moral dignity. . . . That his cannot be the language of the imagination must have necessarily followed from this, that there is not a single image from Nature in the whole body of his works; and in his translation from Vergil whenever Vergil can be fairly said

to have had his *eye* upon his object, Dryden always spoils the passage.

A final convolution of paradox is implied by Wordsworth's judgment: that is, that Dryden's translations finally say less about what he is translating than about Dryden himself. This, in a context less invidious to Dryden, is what Tennyson uses Drydenian translation to demonstrate. As Hallam Tennyson wrote in his memoir of his father, apropos translations of lines from the first book of *The Iliad* by both Dryden and Pope:

> "What a difference," my father would add, "between Pope's little poisonous barbs, and Dryden's strong invective! And how much more real poetic force there is in Dryden!
> "Look at Pope:
> 'He said, observant of the blue-eyed maid,
> Then in the sheath return'd the shining blade':
> Then at Dryden:
> 'He said: with surly faith observed her word
> And in the sheath reluctant plunged the sword.'"

Dryden's "plunged the sword" does seem more dynamic than Pope's "return'd the shining blade"; but the comparison refers entirely to the verbal modes of Dryden and Pope, not to the rendering of the original.

All such paradoxes are the eddies and whirlpools of a continuing current: the untranslatability of poetic essence. This fact, that translations of poetry are invariably and without exception vitiated by the principle of attenuation, can be extrapolated for still larger structures of culture and even for culture as such. The relation of meaning by experience to structures of culture is the same as the relation of lyric poetry to translation. Just as in a true lyric poem a part can be successfully translated and a part cannot, although it is the quest for the part that cannot that imparts the urge to translate in the first place, just so do primary meanings and transcendent meanings relate to meanings by equivalence. The vast activity of cultural equivalence is successful in translating primary meanings, which correspond to the words of the poem and its statement of fact, but unsuccessful in its attempt to translate transcendent meanings, which correspond to the inner spirit of the poem. Attenuated translation is the paradigm of one large aspect of cultural movement.

Take Augustine as example. We marvel at his brilliant mind and great heart, flaming out to us from the immense otherness of the cultural situation of the late fourth and early fifth centuries of this era. The enormous intellectual force that went into his treatises on the city of God, on the Trinity, on music—in truth well over two hundred works issued from his pen—is almost wholly enlisted in the service of the Christian religion. Yet not only all these treatises but the Christian religion itself were schematisms of meaning by equivalence. They were translating the meanings by experience that Augustine records in his *Confessions*. Of those meanings he succeeds in translating only the primary meanings. The transcendent meanings forming the motive core that constituted and gave cultural direction to his deep humanity and wonderful ardor of spirit are only hinted at; indicated, not translated.

One such scene of indication is the exquisite dialogue with Monica at Ostia shortly before her death:

> The day now approaching whereon she was to depart this life (which day Thou well knewest, we knew not), it came to pass . . . that she and I stood alone, leaning in a certain window, looking into the garden of the house where now we lay, at Ostia; where removed from the din of men, we were resting from the fatigues of a long journey. . . . We were discoursing then together, alone, very sweetly; and forgetting those things which are behind, and reaching forth unto those things which are before, we were enquiring between ourselves in the presence of the Truth, which thou Art, of what sort the eternal life of the saints was to be. . . . And . . . our discourse was brought to that point, that the very highest delight of the earthly senses, in the very purest material light, was, in respect of the sweetness of that life, not only not worthy of comparison, but not even of mention; . . . yea, we were soaring higher yet, by in-

ward musing, and discourse, and admiring of Thy works. . . .
And while we were discoursing and panting after Wisdom, we
slightly touched on her with the whole effort of our heart. . . .

Though the passage seeks its transcendence within the framework of
the Christian religion, its inner spirit is that same human exaltation
we find in those supreme lines in *Romeo and Juliet* where, after the
lovers' single night together, Romeo must part forever from his
bride. "O, think'st thou we shall ever meet again?" asks Juliet.
Romeo's reply is ineffably wonderful:

> I doubt it not; and all these woes shall serve
> For sweet discourses in our time to come

The similarity of the two displacements is notable. Both cast
present woes and the implied limitations of the present into a posited
future where the threat of mutability is cancelled. The changing of
"all these woes" to the "sweet discourses" of the future purges the
anxiety of the present state: the discourses are sweet because the woes
are only a playful remembrance. The human intensity of the ideal
togetherness that is projected into happiness absolute, however, re-
capitulates past happiness—where else could such intensity arise?
In both cases the transcendent meaning that makes the futurity wonderful is already present in the projecting situation.

But this transcendent meaning in *Romeo and Juliet,* which is
similar in structure to that of Augustine and Monica, is not, as theirs
is, set in the matrix of the Christian religion. The Christian faith of
Augustine is the "I doubt it not" of Romeo; yet the human import is
the same. By the same token, the Christian religion was not the essence, but rather an attempt at a translation, of Augustine's own
burning sense of meaning in life. Indeed, Augustine was really the
same—already having experienced transcendent meaning—before
his conversion as he was after (which is perhaps the reason that the
conversion itself was such a slow and long-deferred process). Thus,
as early as the second book of the *Confessions,* where he records
himself as scarcely more than a boy, he remembers the unique ardor
of his commitment to truth: "Truth! Truth! How the very marrow of
my soul within me yearned for it as they dinned it in my ears over

and over again!" In that same section he recalls his first meeting with a book that inspired him:

> The prescribed course of study brought me to a work by an author named Cicero, whose writing nearly everyone admires. . . . The title of the book is *Hortensius* and it recommends the reader to study philosophy. It altered my outlook on life. . . . In Cicero's book was his advice not simply to admire one or another of the schools of philosophy, but to love wisdom itself, whatever it might be, and to search for it, pursue it, hold it, and embrace it firmly. These were the words that excited me and set me burning with fire. . . .

But the book could only have set him burning with fire because his soul had already experienced the transcendent meaning of which we speak.

The principle at issue here obtains everywhere, even in the most unlikely expressions of high culture. As extreme instance, take Rabelais. On the surface, no one can seem farther from transcendent possibility; the human spectacle is for Rabelais so irresistibly low and ludicrous that there is hardly a subject he can approach without a fecal grin that promptly widens into hilariously destructive laughter. The motto on the Abbaye de Theleme, "FAY CE QUE VOULDRAS"— "Do what you want"—seems to level every possible structure of values; and the Abbaye itself represents a direct attack on the social institution of the church. But in truth Rabelais' current of mirth erodes the foundations of every hierarchical structure it encounters; indeed, so subversive of all established reverence is his tendency that if one accepts Michelet's view that the French Revolution had for centuries been rolling inevitably towards the explosion of 1789, then Rabelais, a quarter of a millennium earlier, must be accepted as a major harbinger of that explosion.

His cornucopian repetitions of excremental and copulative reference serve to reduce human hierarchies to the equality of universal animal functions. Episode after episode crumbles all dignity into tropes of grotesquerie. The transcendence accorded the ideal of kingship in the Renaissance is washed away by the ludicrous spectacle of the choleric King Picrochole, waging heroic war over the theft of some cakes from his bakers, and finally reduced, still furious, to the status of porter at Lyon. The portentous King Anarche, similarly, is ludicrously diminished to a crier of green sauce, as Rabelais superimposes on the dignity of kingship his subversively leveling language: "These accursed kings," says Pantagruel, "are absolute dolts. They know nothing, and they're good for nothing except harming their poor subjects, and troubling the whole world with wars, for their wicked and detestable pleasure. I mean to put him to a trade, and make him a hawker of green sauce."

Other structures of transcendence fare no better. When the learned Janotus de Bragmardo is sent to plead for the bells of Notre Dame that Gargantua has taken away, he foreshadows both Pope's Sir Plume in the anti-eloquence of his pleading and Shakespeare's Holofernes (the name also of Gargantua's tutor) in his macaronic obfuscations: "A hem, hm, hm! G'day, sir, and g'day to *vobis*, gentlemen. It would only be right if you were to give us back the bells, for we are greatly in need of them. H'm, h'm, hasch! . . . Well now, *de parte Dei, date nobis clochas nostras* [for God's sake give us our bells]."

But even this hilarious send-up of eloquence and classical learning must take second rank to Rabelais' inspired imagination in the contest of learning between Panurge and Thaumaste, where the word-torrents of scholarship are dammed into ludicrous pantomime:

> Then Panurge struck one hand against the other and blew in his palm. After which he once more thrust the forefinger of his right hand into the ring made by his left, pushing it in and drawing it out several times. Then he stuck out his chin and looked intently at Thaumaste. . . . Thaumaste now began to sweat great drops. . . . Then he got an idea, and put all the nails of his left hand against those of his right, opening his fingers in a semi-circular fashion, and raised his hands as high as he could in this attitude.

This is hilarity that may have peers in world literature, but assuredly no superiors.

And yet right in the middle of the maelstrom of subversion generated by Rabelais' comic genius, there is, remarkably, an indication of the third kind of meaning that the swirling humor not only does not erode but does not even touch. The place is the letter of Gargantua to Pantagruel. That here for once there is no mirth, nor even the hint of mirth, indicates the approach to a region of transcendent meaning:

> Among the gifts, graces, and prerogatives with which the Sovereign Creator, God Almighty, endowed and embellished human nature in the beginning, one seems to me to stand alone, and to excel all others; that is the one by which we can, in this mortal state, acquire a kind of immortality and, in the course of this transitory life, perpetuate our name and seed; which we do by lineage sprung from lawful marriage. By this means there is in some sort restored to us what was taken from us by the sin of our first parents, who were told that, because they had not been obedient to the commandment of God the Creator, they would die, and that by death would be brought to nothing that magnificent form in which men had been created.

The intense seriousness is maintained as the letter enunciates the ideal of Renaissance learning that was arising from the mists of medieval experience:

> Indeed, the times were still dark, and mankind were perpetually reminded of the miseries and disasters wrought by the Goths, who had destroyed all sound scholarship. But . . . learning has been restored in my age to its former dignity and enlightenment. . . . Now every method of teaching has been restored, and the study of languages has been revived: of Greek, without which it is disgraceful for a man to call himself a scholar, and of Hebrew, Chaldean, and Latin. . . . The whole world is full of learned men, of very erudite tutors, and of most extensive libraries. . . .

The vision of the renewal of learning is followed by the counsel to participate in this ideal:

> It is my earnest wish that you shall become a perfect master of languages. First of Greek, as Quintilian advises; secondly, of Latin; and then of Hebrew, on account of the Holy Scrip-

tures . . . and I would have you model your Greek style on
Plato's and your Latin on that of Cicero. . . . Of the liberal
arts, geometry, arithmetic, and music, I gave you some smat-
tering . . . go on and learn the rest. . . . Of Civil Law I would
have you learn the best texts by heart, and relate them to the art
of philosophy. And as for Nature's works, I should like you to
give careful attention to that too; so that there may be no sea,
river, or spring of which you do not know the fish. All the birds
of the air, all the trees, shrubs, and bushes of the forest . . . let
none of them be unknown to you.

It is this fleetingly glimpsed star of transcendence that moves the
vast sea of Rabelaisian humor, and all that humor is likewise the attenuated translation of a vision that cannot be expressed; is, indeed,
an attempt ultimately to translate that vision into knowledge, which
was not then so overwhelming, rather than into meaning.

That Rabelais located the possibilities of transcendence in the acquirement of knowledge does in truth mark a major difference between his situation and our own. Only in more recent times has it
become apparent, at least to the discerning, that the aim of culture
cannot possibly be knowledge—though this is what the existence of
research libraries and university curricula, no less than of the con-
ventions of scholarship (fields, topics, footnotes, and the rest), even
now proudly assumes. For if it were knowledge, as still seemed
feasible in the early Renaissance, culture would by now long since
have collapsed. Indeed, it would have collapsed before 1858, when
Emerson, as noted above, took despairing survey of the immensity
of printed production and the libraries that collected it. Swedenborg
thought that the Last Judgment had occurred in 1757; certainly by
that year knowledge, as goal of culture, had heard its own apocalyptic trumpet.

The aim of culture, however, which persists undisturbed, can only
be meaning, which waxes and wanes but does not accumulate or ex-
plode. And the never-ending flow of translation, both of works from
one language into another and that comprised by the endlessly subtle
transformations of meanings by equivalence, is set in motion by the
quest for meaning, not the quest for knowledge, however much the

institutions of the present-day intellectual establishment may still seem to affirm that it is knowledge that counts.

Yet, though what is commonly known as translation clusters around the principle of attenuation and adequately describes the larger cultural movement from meaning by experience to meaning by equivalence, such translation is not the whole story. Attenuation is the most obvious characteristic of translation but not the only one, and possibly not even the most important one. To complete these arguments about culture, its nature, and its significance, it will be necessary to consider a second principle: impedance. That, translation as impedance, and thereby culture as impedance, will be the subject of the next chapter.

3

SPECIAL
LANGUAGES

The previous chapter has talked—chattered, it may sometimes seem—about the structure of translation as the pattern for the movement of cultural meaning. It noted that translations of poems never reach the essence of the poems, that they are attenuated by their very nature. It suggested that cultural activity is similar to the structure of such translation in that it constantly attempts, and as constantly fails, to express transcendent meanings that are evanescent and indeed limited to the experience of less than everyone. The tendency of what has been said up to now is that all cultural activity is a kind of translation and by that very fact can be no more than a series of approximations to the meanings it attempts to grasp and transmit.

But I suggested at the end of the chapter that translation centering upon the phenomenon of attenuation does not wholly account for cultural activity. An entirely different kind of translational activity, one that centers upon the phenomenon of impedance, must be taken into account if the larger nature of cultural activity is to become clear. It is this second kind of translation, translation as impedance, that this chapter will discuss; for such discussion is necessary as conclusion to these heterodox thoughts about the evacuations of meaning in life and the attempts at the reclamation of meaning by culture.

We may take our departure from a recent book by E. D. Hirsch called *The Philosophy of Composition*. Hirsch has been interested in certain pedagogical problems arising from the necessity of having large numbers of students provide writing samples that must be assessed by many different graders. The specific point with which he has been occupied is how to insure consistency and equity in such varied judgments. Toward that end he has attempted to isolate certain qualitative features of style so that multiple graders could be trained to render approximately equal judgments. Here, however, we are not concerned with the total implications of Hirsch's work but simply with its usefulness as a springboard to the concept of impedance.

In his search for the secret of style, Hirsch concludes that

> there are universal stylistic features in all good prose of every kind and that these features of good style are all reducible to a single principle: One prose style is better than another when it communicates the same meanings as the other does but requires less effort from the reader. Since this stylistic principle is tolerant of every conceivable semantic intention in prose, it does not favor any single prose style. Intentional elegance, intentional obscurity, and intentional lucidity are equally governed by the principle.

Hirsch then gives this single principle a name: "relative readability."

And yet, however willing or even eager we might find ourselves to agree with the criterion of "relative readability," we can accept it only by conceding an exception. This exception moreover, is a weighty one. For it seems, in cultural history, that the more important an intellectual manifestation is, the more difficult it is to grasp. Plato quotes a proverbial saying that "all fine things are difficult" (*Republic* 497D); while Spinoza concludes his *Ethics* with the statement "omnia praeclara tam difficilia quam rara sunt"—"all things excellent are as difficult as they are rare." Recently I was reading a little book by Werner Marx called *Hegel's Phenomenology of Spirit: A Commentary on the Preface and Introduction,* and its opaque pages are justified, in the words of the blurb, by the fact that Hegel's treatise is "considered to be the most difficult text in all of philosophical literature." Be that as it may—counterclaims could certainly be made on behalf of Kant's *Critique of Pure Reason* or Husserl's *Ideas* or Plato's *Parmenides*—the absence of "relative readability" not only does not characterize Hegel alone, but is in fact almost a constant in important cultural manifestation.

For a single instance, only by a heroic stretch can Hirsch's "relative readability" apply to the statements of Wittgenstein's *Tractatus*. "Wittgenstein's first interest," writes Gilbert Ryle,

> has been in the logic of mathematics and thence in the logical paradoxes which were the big leak in the dry dock that Frege and Russell had built. He was, therefore, equipped and predisposed to squeeze whatever can be significantly said into the few statement-patterns with which the logic of mathematical statements operates. He uses its terminology, its codes, and its abacus-operations in his task of exploring various philosophical issues, and, above all, his own master-issue, that of the nature of philosophizing itself. In consequence, the *Tractatus* is, in large measure, a closed book to those who lack this technical equipment. Few people can read it without feeling that something important is happening; but few experts, even, can say what is happening.

If by Hirsch's criterion of "relative readability" we find that the underlying assumption about a style is that it is a formation of language that attempts to facilitate communication, then the *Tractatus*, which is here described as "in large measure, a closed book" to most of us, and a book in which "few experts, even, can say what is happening," would seem to be composed not primarily upon the principle of "relative readability" but rather upon a principle of hindered readability. Wittgenstein's special form of communication entails not a making of transparency but a making of impedance.

This truth is bulwarked by the very existence of, say, Max Black's *A Companion to Wittgenstein's Tractatus*, which itself runs to nearly 450 pages and contains the following assurance:

> No philosophical classic is harder to master. According to Wittgenstein himself, it was misunderstood by Russell, Moore and Frege. . . . The reader's difficulty is partly due to the extreme compression of Wittgenstein's often oracular remarks. Within a span of some twenty thousand words there are comments on the nature of the universe and the essence of language, important contributions to the foundations of logic and mathematics, penetrating criticisms of the work of Frege and

Russell, the outlines of a theory of probability, revolutionary ideas about philosophical method, not to mention occasional remarks about philosophy of science, ethics, religion, and mysticism. Wittgenstein disliked circumlocution and found it painful to elaborate thoughts that were no longer fresh; his ideas would be valuable, he felt, only for those who had had similar ideas and could trace their implications unaided. . . . A serious reader must labour strenuously to reconstruct Wittgenstein's thoughts from cryptic and elliptical suggestions, getting what help he can from a succession of images that dazzle as much as they illuminate.

Indeed, Wittgenstein's whole career, if we listen to Ryle's words from another portion of the essay cited above, was built around the principle of impedance. "In 1947," wrote Ryle in 1951, Wittgenstein "resigned his Chair" at Cambridge:

Besides the *Tractatus,* he published only one article.

In the last twenty years, so far as I know, he published nothing; attended no philosophical conferences; gave no lectures outside Cambridge; corresponded on philosophical subjects with nobody and discouraged the circulation even of notes of his Cambridge lectures and discussions. . . . Yet from his jealously preserved little pond, there have spread waves over the philosophical thinking of the English-speaking world. Philosophers who never met him—and few of us did meet him—can be heard talking philosophy in his tone of voice; and students who can barely spell his name now wrinkle up their noses at things which had a bad smell for him.

Perhaps if enough qualifications were introduced, some version of Hirsch's universal principle of "relative readability" might be maintained as an at least approximate description of communicative variations such as that represented by the writing and career of Wittgenstein. But we can arrive at a more satisfactory adjudication, I suggest, if we begin by realizing that all written communication is not of the same kind. We can, in fact, distinguish at least five discrete genres of writing. These genres are not arbitrary, but on the contrary are determined by differences in the guiding purpose of their composition. To use the simplest names possible, they may be called *data, notices, story-telling, poetry,* and *truth-telling.* (Though Hirsch speaks only of prose, for our purposes the more comprehensive schematism is desirable.)

The term *data* perhaps requires no elucidation here. Under it and the second term, *notices,* is included perhaps nine-tenths of all writing. A notice is anything from a traffic ticket to an issue of the *New York Times,* from a business letter to the Declaration of Independence. For notices in general Hirsch's criterion of "relative readability" seems to identify stylistic quality. There can, of course, be some overlapping, as when a university diploma combines its function as notice with a certain amount of translational impedance by being written in Latin, and thereby simulates truth-telling. Such overlappings are of great interest to any full-scale development of the distinctions I propose, but for my purposes here it remains true that "relative readability" is a pertinent criterion for stylistic quality in the realm of notice.

The third realm, that of *story-telling*—the name is suggested by Barbara Hardy's study of fictional enterprise called *Tellers and Listeners*—is, again with exceptions and qualifications, also somewhat responsive to the criterion of "relative readability," although it has long been noted that "good" or "bad" style has little to do with novelistic quality. And here, too, there is overlapping, as for instance in *Hamlet,* where the function of story-telling combines with that of truth-telling. Moreover, some kinds of story-telling, *Finnegans Wake* for instance, decisively resist any evaluation in terms of "relative readability."

The fourth realm, *poetry,* is still less bound up with the criterion of "relative readability." On the contrary, a central tenet of Russian Formalism was that poetic language is impeded language. As Victor Shklovsky said in 1917:

Habitualization devours works, clothes, furniture, one's wife, and the fear of war. . . . And art exists that one may recover the sensation of life; it exists to make one feel things, to make the stone *stony*. The technique of art is to make objects "un-familiar," to make forms difficult. . . .

In studying poetic speech in its phonetic and lexical structure as well as in its characteristic distribution of words and in the characteristic thought structures compounded from the words, we find everywhere the artistic trademark—that is, we find material obviously created to remove the automation of perception; the author's purpose is to create the vision which results from that deautomatized perception. . . . The language of poetry is, then, a difficult, roughened, impeded language.

What Shklovsky is saying is very important. Far from being a merely idiosyncratic observation, it goes on the contrary to the very heart of what poetry historically has been: no poet has ever been under any obligation to be clear and readable. Poet after poet, theorist after theorist, has realized that "readability" is not only not necessary to poetry but is in fact antithetical to its interests. "Few poets of the highest class," writes Shelley, "have chosen to exhibit the beauty of their conceptions in its naked truth and splendour." Tennyson, in defending Browning's obscurity, says, "I believe it is a mistake to explain poetry too much." Coleridge, in one of his pregnant notebook jottings, observes that "the elder Languages [were] fitter for Poetry because they expressed only prominent ideas with clearness, other but darkly."

Obscurity is not only natural to poetry but is sought as a chief means of dramatizing the unique nature of the poetic statement, and of emphasizing the rejection of the quotidian chatter of ordinary speech. "Where matters truly solemn and memorable are too much exposed," writes Boccaccio, the office of the poet is "by every effort, to protect as well as he can and remove them from the gaze of the irreverent, that they cheapen not by too much common familiarity." "The more incommensurable and incomprehensible for the understanding a poetic creation may be, the better," said Goethe to Eckermann. Ronsard says that he learned to be a poet by following Jean Dorat, who taught him how "to hide the truth of things" in poetry:

> . . . et de là le vins estre
> Disciple de Dorat, qui long temps fut mon maistre,
> M'apprist la Poësie, et me monstra comment
> On doit feindre et cacher les fables proprement,
> Et à bien desguiser la verité des choses
> D'un fabuleux manteau dont elles sont encloses.

Of course some poems are more readable and clear than others, and some are even limpid, but for the most part it seems to be true that poetry has more of a stake in impeded statement than in transparent statement. Frost, for instance, is usually clear; his meaning, however, is less predictably so. On the other hand, a poet such as John Ashbery is notably obscure, with regard to both statement and meaning. "You say that I want somebody to Elucidate my ideas," writes Blake to a correspondent. "But you ought to know that what is Grand is necessarily obscure to weak men. That which can be made Explicit to the Idiot is not worth my care. The wisest of the Ancients considered what is not too Explicit as the fittest for Instruction because it rouzes the faculties to act." To counter a charge that philosophers are often obscure, Cicero, in *De oratore,* points out that poets are obscure too.

In general, the situation for poetry is well described by John Crowe Ransom:

> It is in no very late stage of a poet's advancement, that his taste rejects a sustained phonetic regularity as something restricted and barren, ontologically defective. Accordingly he is capable of writing smooth meters and then roughening them on purpose. And it must be added . . . that he is capable of writing a clean logical argument, and then of roughening that too, by introducing logical violence into it, and perhaps willful obscurity.

"Willful obscurity": that is the deliberate choice of the poetic mode of writing. Who can give a logical paraphrase of Yeats's "Among School Children"? Who can account for clear and distinct logic in Eliot's *The Waste Land?* Who finds Shelley's "Epipsychidion" easy to read? But can it be said to be more difficult than Collins' "Ode on the Poetical Character"? What about the *Duineser Elegien?*

In line with this volume's resolution to hint and intimate rather than to detail and expand, however, we shall not answer those questions or examine further convolutions of the poetic commitment to translational impedance, rewarding though such development might be. It is rather to *truth-telling* that the remainder of this chapter's discussion of special languages will be devoted.

The term *truth-telling*—which is symmetrically offered by analogy with *story-telling*—denotes a realm where "relative readability" holds no sway whatever, as has perhaps already been suggested by the references to Hegel and Wittgenstein. *Truth-telling* is preferable to a term like *philosophy*, partly because the very invocation of the word *philosophy* constitutes a kind of translational impedance, and partly because such nonphilosophical utterance as oracles and prophecies are also readily included under the simpler term. Oracles and prophecies, we doubtless will agree without further ado, are in their very nature impeded statements. An oracle that did not speak in riddles would not remain long in business (the collection of ancient prophecies known as the "Sibylline Oracles"—purporting to be utterances of Greek Sibyls—was exposed as inauthentic by Renaissance scholarship precisely because, compared to the prophecies in Isaiah, it was too clear and precise to be credible). But philosophy, too, characteristically tells its truth in an impeded structure of special language.

To be sure, some philosophers have sought to write clearly. Locke, for instance, inherited both Descartes' commitment to "clear and distinct ideas" as the measure of knowability and the Royal Society's simplification of language in the quest for scientific truth. He spoke with unfailing contempt of those who were obscure in their presentations. He says, for instance, that we should not be "anxious about the sense" of authors

who Writing but their own Opinions, we are under no greater necessity to know them, than they to know ours. Our good or evil depending not on their Decrees, we may safely be ignorant of their Notions: And therefore in the reading of them, if they do not use their Words with a due clearness and perspicuity, we may lay them aside, and without any injury done them, resolve thus with our selves,

Si non vis intelligi, debes negligi.

His intention in his *Essay Concerning Human Understanding,* he says, was in part to clarify matters and make them less obscure:

'tis Ambition enough to be employed as an Under-Labourer in clearing Ground a little, and removing some of the Rubbish, that lies in the way to Knowledge; which certainly had been very much more advanced in the World, if the Endeavours of ingenious and industrious Men had not been much cumbred with the learned but frivolous use of uncouth, affected, or unintelligible Terms, introduced into the Sciences, and there made an Art of, to that Degree, that Philosophy, which is nothing but the true Knowledge of Things, was thought unfit, or uncapable to be brought into well-bred Company, and polite Conversation. Vague and insignificant Forms of Speech, and Abuse of Language, have so long passed for Mysteries of Science; And hard or misapply'd Words, with little or no meaning, have, by Prescription, such a Right to be mistaken for deep Learning, and heighth of Speculation, that it will not be easie to persuade, either those who speak, or those who hear them, that they are but the Covers of Ignorance, and hindrance of true Knowledge.

Eloquent though this denunciation of obscurity is, however, we realize upon reflection that it is occasioned precisely because Locke believes that the reigning mode among philosophers is in fact obscure.

Moreover, despite these emphatic declarations in favor of clearness—"relative readability," if one wishes—Locke does not himself actually eschew a special language. His style is clear, his diction simple and direct. So his own version of special language cannot be taxed with obscurity of utterance. Yet it nonetheless hides his meaning as effectively as the obscurity it so proudly repudiates. In what then consists Locke's own translational impedance to understanding?

The answer can be indicated by a single word: prolixity. Indeed, Locke himself admits as much:

> If thou findest any thing wanting, I shall be glad, that what I have writ, gives thee any Desire, that I should have gone farther: If it seem too much to thee, thou must blame the Subject; for when I first put Pen to Paper, I thought all I should have to say on the Matter, would have been contained in one sheet of Paper; but the farther I went, the larger Prospect I had: New Discoveries led me still on, and so it grew insensibly to the bulk it now appears in. I will not deny, but possibly it might be reduced to a narrower compass than it is; and that some Parts of it might be contracted: the way it has been writ in, by catches, and many long intervals of Interruption, being apt to cause some Repetitions. But to confess the Truth, I am now too lazie, or too busie to make it shorter.

The "bulk it now appears in" has always been an effective bar to the conquest of *An Essay Concerning Human Understanding.* Although almost every intellectual has some idea of the general outlines of Locke's position, and many have read the first two or three chapters of the first book—forty pages, say—not one in a hundred has actually read the treatise through, and only a few specialists have mastered the ramified details of its argument. The book's text runs to 721 pages in the standard modern edition, and such formidable extension proves no less effective an impedance than do the obscurest or most stipulative philosophical vocabulary and syntax.

Hume presents a variant of the same kind of philosophical impedance. Like Locke, he is clear; indeed, he is even graceful in his style and diction. But like Locke, he is prolix. His chief work, *A Treatise of Human Nature,* runs to 662 pages in the standard modern edition, even though like Locke's *Essay,* its truth could conceivably be "contained in one sheet of Paper." Hume's prolixity has a special form, that of the eddy. Any important statement occurs not once but repeatedly, as Hume eddies round and round in his statement. For instance, I once had occasion to quote Hume's tenet that "there is no object, which implies the existence of any other if we consider these objects in themselves." But I neglected to jot down the page number.

As a result, when I came to look for the citation for a footnote reference, I was unable to find it and eventually had to delegate the task to the fresh eyes of a philosopher friend. My own search, however, had proved instructive in that though I was not able to find that precise declaration, I must have found a dozen or more statements almost identical in their import and only slightly different in wording. Some figures combine devices to form their special languages. Husserl, for instance, combines prolixity, eddying, difficult syntax, and stipulative idiosyncrasy of diction to achieve a maximum impedance. At all events, the prevailing mode has always been for truth-tellers to employ an impeded utterance of some kind, a special language that succeeds in holding back rather than revealing their truth. Heraclitus, the first great philosopher of the Western tradition, was called *skoteinos*—dark or obscure—by classical antiquity. Even more deserving of the adjective is that ancient repository of Chinese thought called the *I Ching*. Jesus, the most influential truth-teller of all, characteristically spoke in parables, with the avowed intention not of revealing but of obscuring his truth: "Give not that which is holy unto the dogs, neither cast ye your pearls before swine." That statement occurs in Matthew 7:6. In Matthew 13:9–13, we read further:

> Who hath ears to hear, let him hear.
> And the disciples came, and said unto him, Why speakest thou unto them in parables?
> He answered and said unto them, Because it is given unto you to know the mysteries of the kingdom of heaven, but to them it is not given.
> For whosoever hath, to him shall be given, and he shall have more abundance; but whosoever hath not, from him shall be taken away even that he hath.
> Therefore speak I to them in parables: because they seeing see not; and hearing they hear not, neither do they understand.

The words of Jesus here quoted constitute an absolute norm for the interests of truth-telling. If we look from Jesus to the other most influential truth-teller of antiquity, that is, to Plato, we find impeded translation as much or even more an ineradicable characteristic of the mode of presentation. First of all, the Platonic devices of Socratic persona, conflicting dialogical interests, and endemic playfulness have always made it difficult to say just what were Plato's own opinions. To cite a single example, the classical commentator John Burnet believed that only in the dialogue called *Nomoi* (*Laws*) could Plato's own doctrine be found. And Augustine complained in *The City of God* that "the fact is that Plato makes a point of preserving the manner of his master Socrates, whom he introduces as a disputant in his books. It is well known that Socrates was in the habit of concealing his knowledge, or his beliefs; and Plato approved of that habit. The result is that it is not easy to discover his own opinions even on important matters." Augustine's observation has been repeated at intervals throughout the whole course of Western culture. For a single instance, Pico della Mirandola, in his *Heptaplus*, notes that "Plato hid his beliefs with masks of allegory, a veil of myths, mathematical images, and obscure disclosures of late events, so that he himself declared in his *Epistles* that from what he wrote no one would clearly understand his ideas on divine things."

Still more decisively, moreover, Plato impeded the communication of his truth by dividing his statement into an exoteric, or written doctrine, and an esoteric, or unwritten doctrine; and it is a task for every serious commentator of Platonic thought to try to assess the nature and importance of the unwritten doctrine in its relation to the works we actually have. Plato refers to the division in his seventh *Epistle;* and in the *Phaedrus* Socrates is represented as quoting the Egyptian god Thamus as saying to Theuth, the inventor of writing, that writing is ascribed "a power the opposite of that which it really possesses," and that Theuth has "invented an elixir not of memory, but of reminding; and you offer your pupils the appearance of true wisdom." "He who thinks, then," continues this voice for Socrates, "that he has left behind him any art in writing, and he who receives it in the belief that anything in writing will be clear and certain, would be an utterly simple person" (275C).

If we seek to understand the seemingly contradictory fact that those with the deepest truth to offer are as much concerned to withhold or obscure as to reveal that truth, we will find ourselves led, I suggest, to a threefold solution for the paradox. The first part of the solution is that an impeded special language serves the interests of the author's reputation. Obscurity repels frivolous or hostile readers but captures serious ones. Blake, Derrida, and Kant present an opaque surface to careless or merely cursory inspection; a denunciation of them as obscure, in the absence of really knowing what they say, recoils upon the denouncer. On the other hand, whenever the time, effort, and thought necessary to understand them are put forth, there is an almost invariable tendency to protect such an investment. To expend effort is ipso facto to be converted.

The second part of the solution is that truth-telling is habitually translated into a special language that impedes understanding because no truth is ever the whole truth. Walter Benjamin, in his essay called "On Language as Such and on the Language of Man," states the matter as well as anyone:

> Within all linguistic formation a conflict is waged between what is expressed and expressible and what is inexpressible and unexpressed. On considering this conflict one sees, in the perspective of the inexpressible, at the same time the last mental entity. Now it is clear that in the equation of mental and linguistic being the notion of an inverse proportionality between the two is disputed. For this latter thesis runs: the deeper, that is, the more existent and real the mind, the more it is inexpressible and unexpressed.

Benjamin's formulation accords with Plato's belief. Plato writes in his seventh *Epistle* (which almost all scholars now consider to be genuine) that he "certainly has composed no work" in regard to the subject to which he devotes himself, "nor shall I ever do so in the future, for there is no way of putting it in words like other studies. Acquaintance with it must come rather after a long period of attendance on instruction in the subject itself and of close companionship, when, suddenly, like a blaze kindled by a leaping spark, it is generated in the soul and at once becomes self-sustaining." Truth, in other words, is not a transferable object, or indeed an object at all; and by that same token it is not a communicable entity but a vector of thought and experience, a product of process inseparable from that process. And this is the third solution of the paradox of special language that impedes understanding of the deepest truth: the sanctity of process must be retained, or else the truth understood is not the real truth. The truth must be earned, not simply read. Only by a technique that defers the approach to truth can the original rocky path to truth be simulated. "This book," says Wittgenstein in the first sentence of the preface to the *Tractatus Logico-Philosophicus,* "will perhaps only be understood by those who have themselves already thought the thoughts which are expressed in it—or similar thoughts." Only by an impeded process of earned understanding does one grasp truth in its "truthiness."

That is the triple secret of special languages for truth-telling. Yet behind this secret in three parts lies one still more arcane. "No serious man," summarizes Plato, "will ever think of writing about serious realities for the general public so as to make them a prey to envy and perplexity. In a word, it is an inevitable conclusion from this that when anyone sees anywhere the written work of anyone, whether that of a lawgiver in his laws or whatever it may be in some other form, the subject treated cannot have been his most serious concern—that is, if he himself is a serious man." To transpose this culminating statement into the contentions put forward by this volume, written works contain meanings by equivalences only. The third kind of meaning, which alone is essential, cannot be verbally set forth.

In order to negate the possible objection that these points pertain only to ancient modes of conceiving, we may turn at some length to a more modern example. None could be more fitting than Kant's masterpiece, the *Kritik der reinen Vernunft* or *Critique of Pure Reason;* for as J. H. Randall says, "Kant has been without question the most influential modern philosopher." Yet as Norman Kemp Smith observes, the *Critique of Pure Reason* "is more obscure and difficult than even a metaphysical treatise has any right to be. The difficulties are not merely due to defects of exposition; they multiply rather than diminish upon detailed study." Interestingly enough, the prestige of Kant's great work stands in almost precise correlation to its difficulty. Proust nominates as one of the touchstones of true culture the mastering of the *Critique of Pure Reason,* and I well remember, as a boy in my early teens, first hearing of the work because it was named in a newspaper article reporting the results of an intellectual poll that selected the ten greatest books in the history of mankind.

But the difficulty is as legendary as the prestige. Schiller, for random example, circled about the volume for years before daring to plunge in. On March 3, 1791, he writes to his friend Körner: "You probably can't guess what I'm reading and studying. Nothing worse than Kant. His *Critique of Judgment* . . . has aroused in me the greatest longing to work myself deeper and deeper into his philosophy. With my small acquaintance with philosophical systems the *Critiques of Reason* . . . are for the present still too difficult for me and take too much time." Kant's contemporary, the philosopher Moses Mendelssohn, wrote to a correspondent on January 5, 1784, admitting that "I don't understand" the *Critique of Pure Reason:* "The summary that Mr. Garve published in the *Bibliothek* is clear to me, but other people say that Garve himself didn't understand Kant properly." Kant, for his part, wrote Garve and cheerfully announced: "I must admit that I have not counted on an immediately favorable reception of my work. That could not be, since the expression of my ideas—ideas that I had been working out painstakingly for twelve years in succession—was not worked out sufficiently to be generally understandable."

And yet the difficulty of the *Critique of Pure Reason* was not the result of an inadequate mastery of German style on Kant's part. On the contrary, Windelband notes that Kant's "earlier 'precritical' works are distinguished by easy-flowing, graceful presentation. . . . His later works show the laboriousness of his thought . . . both in the form of the investigation, with its circumstantial heaviness and artificial architectonic structure, and the formation of his sentences, which are highly involved, and frequently interrupted by restriction." Heine makes the same observation. "*The Critique of Pure Reason,*" he says, "is Kant's principal work. . . . With regard to style, Kant merits severer censure than any other philosopher, more especially when we compare this with his former and better manner of writing."

If we are willing to agree that Kant has translated his discourse in the *Critique of Pure Reason* into a special language that constitutes an impedance to the statement of his thought, we will naturally be interested in both the etiology and the teleology of the process. First of all, we must dismiss the most obvious explanation offered by Kant himself. He tells Mendelssohn on August 16, 1783, that the work is "the outcome of reflection that had occupied me for a period of at least twelve years" but that he had "brought it to completion in the greatest haste within some four to five months, giving the closest attention to the content, but with little thought of the exposition or of rendering it easy of comprehension by the reader—a decision which I have never regretted, since otherwise, had I any longer delayed, and sought to give it a more popular form, the work would probably never have been completed at all." This was the same explanation he had proffered Garve a fortnight earlier:

> The exposition of the materials that for more than twelve successive years I had been carefully maturing, was not composed in a sufficiently suitable manner for general comprehension. For the perfecting of its exposition several years would have been required, whereas I brought it to completion in some four or five months, in the fear that, on longer delay, so prolonged a labor might become burdensome, and that my increasing years . . . would perhaps incapacitate me.

And yet we may well doubt whether Kant was being entirely candid, or at all events whether he recognized all aspects of what he had actually done. For instance, though the *Critique of Pure Reason* was published in 1781, Kant lived until 1804 and continued in high publishing productivity for more than a decade beyond the appearance of his great work. Furthermore, it hardly sounds convincing to claim that a popular exposition would have been more onerous to compose than what we actually have. "To the general plan, based upon logical principles," says Norman Kemp Smith, "Kant has himself given the title, architectonic; and he carries it through with a thoroughness to which all other considerations, and even at times those of sound reasoning, are made to give way. . . . He lovingly elaborates even its minor detail, and is rewarded by a framework so extremely complicated that the most heterogeneous contents can be tidily arranged, side by side, in its many compartments."

Moreover, not only did Kant in fact produce a popular exposition of his thought—the *Prolegomena to Any Future Metaphysics*, written promptly thereafter in 1783—but when Fichte later ventured to take up Kant's own inconclusive early statements and talk about supplying a completed form for the critical philosophy, Kant rejected him in 1797 in terms indicating that what he had produced in 1781 and in the second edition of 1787 was in fact what he had wanted to produce: "the *Critique of Pure Reason*," he says in censorious response to Fichte, "is the best criterion of the truth of philosophy"; and he continues: "no change of meanings, no subsequent improvements, no philosophical system formed in a different way, can supersede it; rather . . . the system of critical philosophy, resting upon a fully secured base, fortified for ever, is indispensable to the highest purposes of mankind for all ages to come."

So Kant eventually realized that the special language of the *Critique of Pure Reason* was exactly the language his purposes required. As to the etiology of that language, we may look to a letter from Kant to Markus Herz on February 21, 1772, some nine years before the appearance of the volume. There Kant wrote about the "key to the whole secret of hitherto obscure metaphysics," and said that it lay in the answer to the question "What is the ground of the relation of that in us which we call 'representation' to the object?" After further discussion, he says that "now I am in a position to bring out a 'Critique of Pure Reason' that will deal with the nature of theoretical as well as practical knowledge. . . . With respect to the first part, I should be in a position to publish it within three months." More than a year later, near the end of 1773, he wrote Herz again: "I doubt that many have tried to formulate and carry out to completion an entirely new conceptual science. You can hardly imagine how much time and effort this project requires, considering the method, the divisions, the search for exactly appropriate terms." And if this statement does not invalidate the latter explanations to Mendelssohn and Garve, surely we must admit that a subsequent one does. For on November 24, 1776, Kant wrote to Herz once more. "It must be possible," he said,

> to survey the field of pure reason, that is, of judgments that are independent of all empirical principles, since this lies a priori

in ourselves. . . . What we need in order to indicate the divisions, limits, and the whole content of that field, according to secure principles [are] a critique, a discipline, a canon, and an architectonic of *pure reason,* a formal science . . . that needs for its foundations an entirely special technical vocabulary.

"An entirely special technical vocabulary"—"ganz eigener technischer Ausdrücke"—with that phrase, and the earlier declaration about "exactly appropriate terms," Kant's clear intention to use special language becomes apparent. Indeed, in 1783 he dismisses the criticism of a "lack of popular appeal" with the argument that such a criticism "can in fact be made of every philosophical writing," and in a note he proceeds to defend himself against "the charge that my innovations of language and my impenetrable obscurity cause my readers unnecessary difficulty in grasping my ideas."

So the truth Kant tells is clothed in a special language of legendary difficulty. Indeed, the difficulty of his great work has generated an entire field of philosophical elucidations that have themselves become parts of our culture: the vast commentaries of Hans Vaihinger in German, Herman de Vleeschauwer in French, Edward Caird, Norman Kemp Smith, and H. J. Paton in English, are not only marvels of analysis but abiding monuments to their authors as well.

We may well conclude, therefore, that an important truth lies behind the impeding veil of Kant's special language. What can that truth be? First of all, it must be a very "truthy" truth. As Heidegger tirelessly reminds us, truth is the Greek *alētheia*—that which is unconcealed. A truth that corresponds to the Greek meaning of the word, therefore, would be authentic only if it were grasped by an act of unveiling. Special language provides the veil necessary to truth, and the penetration of that special language is the unveiling by which truth is understood. Indeed, as Heidegger insists:

We know from Heraclitus and Parmenides that the unconcealment of being is not simply given. Unconcealment occurs only when it is achieved by work: the work of the word in poetry, the work of stone in temple and statue, the work of the word in thought. (In accordance with what has been said above, "work" is to be taken here in the *Greek* sense of *ergon,* the creation that discloses the truth of something that is present.)

But to create the disclosure of truth, the *ergon* must have that on which to work, a resistance, so to speak, by which it gains traction, and that resistance is supplied by the impedance of special language. And yet the essential concealment of truth prior to its apprehension as unconcealing not only defines *alētheia;* it also masks from us a startling truth about truth—what one is tempted to call, with apologies to Hannah Arendt, the banality of truth. Perhaps a less charged description would be provided by a phrase such as "the universal availability of truth." Does not Montaigne imply as much by his famous statement: "chaque homme porte la forme entiere de l'humaine condition"—"each man bears the entire form of the human condition?" But even the phrase "the universal availability of truth" needs modification. For though truth is available to anyone, it is actually known only to the few—hence the recurrence of formulas such as Jesus' "who hath ears to hear, let him hear," and his further statement "they seeing see not; and hearing they hear not."

What then is Kant's truth? We must distinguish between the truth that might be summarized in a history of philosophy and the motive truth that caused him to write the *Critique of Pure Reason* in the first place (Richard Rorty has urged that philosophy should reorient itself away from "discovering truth" to "continuing a conversation"; in such a context, all thirty-one volumes of the standard edition of Kant can be seen as tactics "to keep the conversation going": Kant's "truth" lies outside them). The summarized truth is actually a translation, a meaning by equivalence. But the motive truth can only be an apprehension of the third kind of meaning discussed in the previous chapter.

For instance, Nietzsche provides a succinct answer to the question "What is Kant's truth?" It is, he says, "subterranean Christianity." In our own century, A. C. Ewing, in his *Short Commentary on Kant's Critique of Pure Reason,* categorically agrees: "The main thing which Kant thought his work accomplished was to make religion and ethics for ever secure against the skeptic. . . . However the ultimate end which Kant thought that he served is kept far enough away from the means, so that many have been greatly influenced by the Critique who had little sympathy with the purpose I have just mentioned."

But Christianity, even "subterranean" Christianity, does not really tell us what Kant's truth was, for Christianity is itself a translation; its schematism is merely meaning by equivalence. Indeed, Kant's truth has been indicated by others in terms alternative to Christianity. Schopenhauer, for instance, says,

> If Kant's teaching, and since Kant's time, that of Plato, had ever been properly understood and grasped, if men had truly and earnestly reflected on the inner meaning and content . . . of the two great masters . . . they could not have failed long ago to discover how much the two great sages agree, and that the true significance, the aim, of both teachings is absolutely the same.

In our own century, Richard Kroner, in his magisterial treatise *Von Kant bis Hegel*, categorically agrees: "The Kantian philosophy, leaving aside all those contexts in which it relates to its immediate predecessors, can be regarded as a renewal of Platonic idealism from out of the German mind."

And yet if we wish to translate Kant's truth into Plato's truth, we then simply recast our question: What is Plato's truth? Karl Jaspers, in words quoted at the very beginning of this book, provides an answer. "Plato," he says, "created a written work that for depth and greatness has no equal in all the history of philosophy." "And yet," continues Jaspers, "in his own judgment this lifework consisted merely of intimations and reminiscences." It consisted, that is to say, of attempts to convey and to conceal the third kind of meaning, which I have called transcendent meaning. His twenty-seven dialogues are discursive translations of—that is, attempts to indicate at the same time that they demonstrate the nonequivalence of—this essential meaning, which alone has meaning in itself.

The fact that one must speak of Plato's dialogues as a plural, as indeed is the case with the work of all truth-tellers and all poets, witnesses the inevitable formation of this paradoxical structure. The plurality of efforts indicates the attenuated success of every singular effort. If one could tell the full truth or compose the perfect poem—

translate the third kind of meaning into equivalence—then only one dialogue or one poem would be necessary. But one is never enough; each effort is only an approximation; the truth-teller or poet must always try again. Each poet, so to speak, writes his poem over and over again. Shelley believed that all poets were contributing to a single, vast, but not yet realized poem; Schelling thought that all philosophers were contributing to the formation of one philosophy. Certainly each poet and each truth-teller seems driven by a kind of repetition compulsion dictated by the inadequacy of every effort to incorporate the meanings that alone have meaning. "Poem after poem in *Lyrical Ballads 1800*," runs a statement in Heather Glen's *Vision and Disenchantment: Blake's* Songs *and Wordsworth's* Lyrical Ballads, "suggests that the most significant experience is essentially private and noncommunicable."

But what exactly did Plato experience? No one can say—say exactly, that is. Such meanings are not equivalent. I like to think that I myself have some glimmering, by analogy with my own intensive experience. Whatever Plato's experience was, it was unitary and transcendent, an intensive shape of the same kind as the examples of transcendent meaning pointed to in the previous chapter. Plato refers to it at *Phaedrus* 249B–250C:

> For only the soul that has beheld truth may enter into this our human form—seeing that man must needs understand the language of forms, passing from a plurality of perceptions to a unity gathered together by reasoning—and such understanding is a recollection of those things which our souls beheld aforetime as they journeyed with their god, looking down upon the things which now we suppose to be, and gazing up to that which truly is.
>
> Therefore it is meet and right that the soul of the philosopher alone should recover her wings, for she, as far as may be, is ever near in memory to those things of which a god's nearness unto makes him truly god. Wherefore if a man makes right use of such means of remembrance, and ever approaches to the full vision of the perfect mysteries, he and he alone becomes truly perfect. Standing aside from the busy doings of mankind, and

drawing nigh to the divine, he is rebuked by the multitude as being out of his wits, for they know not that he is possessed by a deity. . . .

Now, as we have said, every soul has, by reason of her nature, had contemplation of true being; . . . but to be put in mind thereof by things here is not easy for every soul. . . . Few indeed are left that can still remember much, but when these discern some likeness of the things yonder, they are amazed, and no longer masters of themselves. . . . Beauty it was ours to see in all its brightness in those days when, amidst that happy company, we beheld with our eyes that blessed vision. . . . Steadfast and blissful were the sights on which we gazed in the moment of final revelation, pure was the light that shone around us, and pure were we, without taint of that prison house by which now we are encompassed, and call a body, fast bound therein as an oyster in its shell.

But did Kant experience something of this kind, too? I suggest that he did, however ill the supposition may seem to accord with his desiccated North German environment and the features of the old age in which we historically know him. In actuality the Teutonic regularity of Kant's life amid the eighteenth-century decorums of central Europe no more precluded transcendent meanings than did the comparable situation of another apostle of Teutonic regularity amid similar eighteenth-century decorums. Bernard Shaw recalls the time when "as a boy, I first breathed the air of transcendental regions at a performance of Mozart's Zauberflöte"; and I have myself felt much the same in studying Kant. After all, are not the very words *transcendental* and *transcendent* indelibly associated with the enterprise of Kant?

We do not see Kant in his youth, when the transcendence of love would have been open to him, nor in his childhood, when the other lode of transcendence might have occupied his perspective. But Schiller, to take only one instance, in his inspired essay on naive and sentimental poetry, which is entirely based on a passage in Kant's *Critique of Judgment,* says of one Kantian emphasis in passing, "Anyone who has learned to admire the author only as a great thinker will be pleased here to come upon a trace of his heart, and be convinced by this discovery of Kant's high philosophical calling (which absolutely requires the combination of both characteristics)." And in his flaming letters on the aesthetic education of mankind, which are also wholly founded on Kant, the ardent Schiller insists on Kant's participation in that "universal availability of truth" invoked above: "Concerning those ideas that predominate in the practical part of the Kantian system it is only the philosophers who are at variance; I am confident of showing that mankind as a whole has from the remotest times been in agreement about them."

That the breath of transcendent meaning that constitutes motive truth is not dependent on the cultural environment is parallel to the fact that it is not large but intensive. The spatial smallness of the motive truth is witnessed by statements of the truth-tellers themselves. As was noted above, Locke once said that "when I first put Pen to Paper, I thought all I should have to say . . . would have been contained in one sheet of Paper." A similar example may be summoned from Kant. Writing to J. H. Lambert on September 2, 1770, almost a dozen years before the *Critique* appeared, Kant said that "for perhaps a year now I believe I have arrived at a position that, I flatter myself, I shall never have to change." He continues: "I could summarize this whole science, as far as its nature, the sources of its judgments, and the method with which one can progress in it are concerned; and this summary could be made in a rather small space, namely, in a few letters." But this statement too is a translation, as would have been the few letters.

If it should seem that the insistence on incommunicable transcendent meanings as the motive truths of philosophy too easily dismisses the actual truth-content of the preponderance of philosophical efforts, perhaps a consideration of three undeniable if generally overlooked obliquities will make that dismissal seem less extreme. First of all, consider the fact that philosophical truth-tellers increasingly cannot tell, or even begin to tell, the truth about any of the great questions of existence; they cannot, indeed, even address the region of truth. Jerome Bruner provides a humorous anecdote that casts this deficiency into dramatic relief. It seems that Bertrand

Russell, late for a dinner engagement at the T. S. Eliots' (Mrs. Eliot supplied the story), hailed a taxicab:

> At the first traffic light, the glass partition shot back, and the driver leaned over and said, "I know who you are. You're Bertrand Russell, the philosopher. I've always wanted to ask a philosopher something. . . ." The light turned green and they drove on further. Next red light, the partition slid back again and Russell asked, "Well, what's the question?" "Tell me; you're a philosopher. What's it all about?"

We realize that the hilarity of the anecdote results from the juxtaposition of the real situation (no modern philosopher has the faintest idea of "what it's all about") against the ideal situation (a questioner should be able to feel perfectly justified in asking a philosopher "What's it all about?"). Anyone who has followed the flight from the great questions that marks many of the philosophical movements of this century, especially those stemming from or allied with the positivism of the Vienna Circle, knows that the truth-telling goals of modern philosophy are modest in the extreme.

Indeed, vital questions are now customarily abandoned to the proponents of other shapes of culture. We now have to look at rather unsatisfactory psycho-biological guesses such as Charles Lumsden and Edward O. Wilson's *Promethean Fire: Reflections on the Origin of Mind,* not at works of "philosophy," if we seek an address to such questions as "Who are we?" and "Where are we going?"; though in the past the question "What's it all about?" was habitually addressed by great thinkers, as in, say, the *Enneads* of Plotinus or the *Ethics* of Spinoza, or even the prophetic books of Blake. The radical shrinking of twentieth-century philosophical boundaries is parallel, in the sphere of truth-telling, to that reshaping downward of mankind's self-image that is signalized by the view put forward by Dostoevsky's devil:

> I maintain that nothing need be destroyed, that we only need to destroy the idea of God in man. . . . As soon as men have all of them denied God . . . the old conception of the universe will

fall of itself . . . and everything will begin anew. Men will unite to take from life all it can give, but only for joy and happiness in the present world. Man will be lifted up with a spirit of divine Titanic pride and the man-god will appear. From hour to hour extending his conquest of nature . . . man will feel such lofty joy from hour to hour in doing it that it will make up for all his old dreams of the joys of heaven. Every one will know that he is mortal and will accept death proudly and serenely like a god. His pride will teach him that it's useless for him to repine at life's being a moment. . . .

The devil's perfervid prescription, indeed, as offered to Ivan Karamazov, sounds very much like that promulgated by Russell's own *Conquest of Happiness*. One feels almost apologetic in pointing out that gods do not have to accept death, proudly, serenely, or otherwise.

Of course the "conquest of nature," if by that we mean the unforeseen effects of scientific and industrial progress, might change the balance of all equations, and even open up new varieties of meaning. At present, however, the onrush of science can hardly be said to have altered the human situation in any essential way. If science were eventually to enable man to circumvent death, that would certainly change things, and new meanings would undoubtedly emerge. But just now a cold view might maintain that science, with the single exception of anesthesia (and possibly vaccination) has not produced anything that constitutes an unequivocal improvement in our lot, and nothing that adds new colors to the spectrum of meaning. New comforts—heated indoor bathrooms rather than primitive outdoor ones, for instance—are existentially trivial, as are telephones, television, automobiles, and the rest. And none is unequivocal even in its limited blessing. Automobiles create jobs and allow us more convenient motion, but they produce junk and blight and pollution, and the highways necessary to their functioning monotonize the countryside; airplanes have supplanted ships to provide more speedy travel, but in doing so they have themselves become cattle cars that ill compare with the luxury and adventure of the old ocean liners. More important advances do not affect existential realities either: better medical care and longer life change little ("Nor love thy Life, nor hate; but what thou liv'st, / Live well, how long or short permit to Heav'n"). And these advances bring negatives in direct ratio to their importance. Fewer children die in infancy, but as a consequence we are faced with the specter of overpopulation. More industrial goods are available to more people, but as a consequence we are threatened with irreparable damage to our environment. And so it goes. It is at present uncertain whether the dramatic unleashing of new sources of power is driving mankind toward the stars or toward oblivion.

Secondly, to return from the role of science to our larger argument about truth-telling, the most extensive portion of philosophical effort simply witnesses that hegemony of the quotidian broached at the end of the first chapter above. Some years ago, I happened to tell Harold Bloom that I was contemplating a charter subscription to the collected works of Heidegger then beginning to be edited. He idly asked me whether it would contain more than a few volumes, mentioning as I recall *Sein und Zeit* and possibly books like *Holzwege* or *Wegmarken,* and I remember his amazement when I told him that to sign up for the subscription would be to sign up for a set of seventy books. Certainly all that Heidegger really had to say was contained in the few works Bloom had in mind; but Heidegger arose every morning during a long professional career, looked in the mirror and saw a face defined as that of a philosopher, went to his university and gave lectures under that public and private definition of his being, and as the days rolled by, the work rolled out, irrespective of truth or inspiration.

To be sure, Heidegger did witness truth and did experience inspiration. Their location, however, was in the realm of the third kind of meaning, outside the consecutive argumentation of his discourse. What motivated Heidegger was the wonder of being, a wonder he pointed to repeatedly but never grasped, as in his posing (with Leibniz) of the first question of philosophy: "To philosophize is to ask 'Why are there things that exist rather than nothing?'" Again, all of Heidegger dwells in the following statement, which glimpses, though it cannot encompass, the third kind of meaning:

Only poetry stands in the same order as philosophy and its thinking, though poetry and thought are not the same thing. . . .

The spirit of poetry (only authentic and great poetry is meant) is essentially superior to the spirit that prevails in all mere sciences. By virtue of this superiority the poet always speaks as though the existing thing were being expressed and invoked for the first time. Poetry, like the thinking of the philosopher, has always so much world space to spare that in it each thing—a tree, a mountain, a house, the cry of a bird—loses all indifference and commonplaceness.

All of Heidegger, still again, dwells in this statement too, which like the other is from his *Einführung in die Metaphysik:*

> How does it stand with being? Can you see being? We see things that are; this chalk for example. But do we see being as we see color and light and shade? Or do we hear, smell, taste, feel being? We hear the motorcycle racing through the street. We hear the grouse gliding through the forest. . . . We hear the flying bird, even though strictly speaking we should say: a grouse is nothing audible, it is no manner of tone that fits into a scale. And so it is with the other senses. We touch velvet, silk; we see them directly as this and that kind of existing thing, the one different from the other. Wherein lies and wherein consists being?

All of Heidegger, yet once more, resides in still another of many possible passages, this one taking up that image of a tree cited in the second chapter above as eliciting the wonder of Blake and of Dostoevsky:

> We stand outside of science. Instead we stand before a tree in bloom, for example—and the tree stands before us. The tree faces us. The tree and we meet one another, as the tree stands there and we stand face to face with it. As we are in this relation of one to the other and before the other, the tree and we *are. . . .* Let us stop here for a moment, as we would to catch our breath before and after a leap. For that is where we are now, men who have leapt out of the familiar realm of science and even, as we shall see, out of the realm of philosophy. And where have we leapt? Perhaps into an abyss? No! . . . A curi-

ous, indeed uncanny thing that we must first leap onto the soil on which we really stand.

But despite his pervasive wonder before being, the consecutive argumentation and linear wordage of Heidegger witness, too, as does the written endeavor of other thinkers, the unceasing dominance of the quotidian.

At another place in *Was heisst Denken?*—which is where the passage just cited occurs—Heidegger points explicitly to the third kind of meaning, which both stands outside communicable meaning and makes actual utterance unsatisfactory:

> No thinker ever has entered into another thinker's solitude. Yet it is only from its solitude that all thinking, in a hidden mode, speaks to the thinking that comes after or that went before. The things that we conceive and assert to be the results of thinking are the misunderstandings to which thinking unavoidably falls victim. Only these things achieve publication as alleged thought, and occupy those who do *not* think.

The statement should be compared to the passage, cited above, from Plato's seventh *Epistle* about the inefficacy of written meaning.

Thirdly, to return to the enumerated reasons for not estimating philosophical truth-content too highly, a cold view of the efforts of truth-tellers would identify the vast majority of all their activity as of no more consequence than a game. I am here thinking only a little of Huizinga, still less of Foucault, and of Wittgenstein scarcely at all, but rather of the skeptical conclusions of an earlier truth-teller, Friedrich Jacobi (whom, significantly, Hegel praised as "ein tief gebildeter Mann"—"a deeply cultured man").

> We know that which is hardly worth knowing, and we find ways of giving our ignorance infinite new forms. . . . Thus we do not perceive that, in the final analysis, we are only playing a game with empty ciphers. . . . This game with our ignorance is certainly the noblest of games, but it is, none the less, clearly seen, only a game with which we pass the time away, rather than truly fulfill it, or attain in it real, essential existence.

Jacobi was here writing in 1811, in his *Von den göttlichen Dingen und ihrer Offenbarung.* A dozen years earlier, in 1799, he had expressed the same cold skepticism in his *Brief an Fichte* (it was Jacobi, incidentally, who coined the word *nihilism,* which has been subsequently so often encountered and was taken up by Nietzsche as the chilling description of the inevitable future form of philosophizing):

> Our sciences, as such, are games which the human intelligence, to pass away the time, devises for itself. Devising these games, the intelligence only organizes its unknowingness, without coming a hair's breadth closer to knowledge of the truth. In a certain sense the mind even gets farther away from the truth, because when so occupied it no longer feels the pressure of unknowingness, even comes to love unknowingness, because that is—infinite; because the game becomes ever more complex, more delightful, huger, more enchanting.

Jacobi in effect agrees with Plato, who despite, or rather because of, the signaling of the third kind of meaning noted above at *Phaedrus* 249B–250C, finds the whole panorama of meaning by equivalence a thing that should not be taken too seriously. As Plato says at *Laws* 803B–D in what I. M. Crombie, in his two volumes called *An Examination of Plato's Doctrines,* terms "a remarkable and haunting passage":

> Man's life is a business that does not deserve to be taken too seriously. . . . What I mean is that man ought to be serious about serious things, and not about trifles, and that while God is the real object of all serious effort, man is constructed . . . as a plaything of God, and that is really the best thing about him. We all, both men and women, should accept this role and spend life in making our play as perfect as possible. . . . What, then, is our right course? We should pass our lives in the playing of certain games—sacrificing, singing, and dancing.

Or doing philosophy.

Philosophy as part of culture, culture as part of life, life as perspective on being, constitute a series of presences stretched out between two absences. The first is indicated by the memory of past meaning; the second, by the hope of reclaiming that meaning. Between these two absences, across the texture of life, the winds of culture blow. Their motion and force are made up, with regard to meaning, of translations; with regard to activity, of repetitions. But it is the third kind of meaning, the absence that resides at both frontiers of these presences, that roils the surface of human existence and propagates the winds that blow.

The incomplete meaning of presence streams toward the vacuum engendered by absence. "Nostalgia is frequent with poets," writes John Crowe Ransom, musing on the topic to which he devoted his life: "The tense of poetry is the past." "Poet of Nature," apostrophizes Shelley of Wordsworth, "thou hast wept to know / That things depart which never may return." Or one may look forward to the hope of restoration rather than back to the memory of loss: "My heart is full of futurity," writes Blake. "Poets," confirms Shelley, "are . . . the mirrors of the gigantic shadows which futurity casts upon the present." In between is existence itself. "Life is a struggle to be what we are not, and to do what we cannot," avers Hazlitt in somber appraisal of that reality.

The hegemony of absence is a cultural constant. Speaking of Marlowe, and specifically of Tamburlaine's "celebrated speech 'What is beauty sayeth my sufferings then?'" Stephen Greenblatt points out that "beauty, like all the goals pursued by the playwright's heroes, always hovers just beyond the reach of human thought and expression. The problem of elusiveness is one of the major preoccupations of Renaissance thinkers from the most moderate to the most radical, from the judicious Hooker to the splendidly injudicious Bruno."

Should we turn from the language of English and American culture to cultural statement in other languages, we find the same disposition of evacuated presence and pregnant absence. "In Chekhov," writes the commentator Richard Gilman, "the past is loss, the future illusion; the present is the painful midpoint between the two, the process through which our illusions become our losses." Again, consider Hölderlin's salute to the third kind of meaning, its rareness, and the largeness of its effect: "Nur zu Zeiten erträgt göttliche Fülle der Mensch / Traum von ihnen is drauf das Leben," he writes—"Only at times does man bear divine fullness / Afterwards life is a dream of those moments." And alongside this signaling of the experience of the third kind of meaning, its evanescence, and its importance, another poetic cry by Hölderlin may confirm Hazlitt's recognition of the emptiness of presence as such: "Aber weh! es wandelt in Nacht, es wohnt, wie im Orkus, / Ohne Göttliches unser Geschlecht"— "But alas! our race wanders in night, dwells as though in Orcus / without the divine."

What the great poet Hölderlin signifies in the language of his art is apprehended too in the language of criticism by his Romantic contemporaries. Actually, *Romantic* is a misnomer for those intense circles at Jena and Berlin that labored to define the nature of poetry and philosophy, for what they were actually attempting to grasp was nothing less than the essence of culture itself. Romanticism as an epoch in sensibility had been flourishing in Germany for decades; such products of so-called "Sturm und Drang" as *Werther* in 1774 or *Die Räuber* in 1781 are in fact the purest Romanticism. On the other hand, what the brothers Schlegel were trying to formulate around the turn of the nineteenth century, though they termed it "Romantic poetry," was, more deeply, the evacuated presence and pregnant absence that actually constitute the subject matter and moving force of culture. Thus, for Friedrich Schlegel "the Romantic mode of poetry" was "ever in process of becoming" ("noch im Werden"): "indeed, that is its real essence, that it eternally only becomes, can never be completed"—"ja dass ist ihr eigentliches Wesen, dass sie ewig nur werden, nie vollendet sein kann." Such poetry includes the whole of culture: it is "a progressive universal poetry"—"eine progressive Universalpoesie"—and "encompasses everything, so long as it is poetic"—"umfasst alles, was nur poetisch ist." Schlegel concludes, significantly, that "in a certain sense all poetry is or ought to be Romantic." Modern poetry, concurred his brother Wilhelm, is a poetry of "longing" ("Sehnsucht"); it balances itself "between remembrance and presentiment" ("zwischen Erinnerung und Ahnung"). Such process of poetry is the process of life itself. "Activity is man's lot," said Kant in an interview with the Russian traveller Karamzin: "He can never be completely content with that which he has, but is always striving to obtain something more."

So there it is. Culture, in this view, is testimony not to our spiritual grandeur but to our existential poverty. "We are, in sum," writes Clifford Geertz in *The Interpretation of Cultures*, "incomplete or unfinished animals who complete or finish ourselves through culture." But Geertz's formulation flatters human life too much. The heterodox view presented in these chapters would force an amendment to his observation. It is agreed that we are incomplete or unfinished animals, from both the anthropologist's perspective and that of this book; but that we complete or finish ourselves through culture is too optimistic a conclusion. For culture primarily witnesses the absence of meaning, not its presence; and the amended form for Geertz's conclusion would accordingly have to be this: "We are, in sum, incomplete or unfinished animals who continually *try to* complete or finish ourselves through culture." But like the Ancient Mariner, no matter how many times we tell our cultural story it must always be told again. The retellings comprise both the cumulative history of culture and proof that our existential failings are never expiated. At least not in this world.

4

THE
WILLING
SUSPENSION
OF
DISBELIEF

The accumulation of culture that results from the necessary repetition of its efforts testifies to the difficulty with which the glimpse of transcendent meanings can be recovered. Every painter paints many pictures; every poet writes many poems. And they do so despite the palpable fact that no more pictures are aesthetically necessary, no more poems are required to fill our hunger for poetry. "When we have Shakespear," says Hazlitt apropos the paradox of continued cultural production, "we do not want more Shakespears; one Milton, one Pope or Dryden, is enough. Have we not plenty of Raphael's, of Rubens's, of Rembrandt's pictures in the world?" He continues: "Who has seen all the fine pictures, or read all the fine poetry, that already exist—and yet till we have done this, what do we want with more?" But the flood of new culture continues with ever-augmenting roar.

Hazlitt is speaking of Shakespeare and Rembrandt; still more overwhelming is the deluge of culture seen from less lofty heights. In an interview reported in the *Boston Review* for February 1986, Harold Bloom takes astonished note of the continuing flood of certain kinds of cultural production: "*BR:* 'What's the value of those second- to ninth-rate critics?' *HB:* 'No value whatsoever. And I repeat one should also ask the question, what is the value of all this bad poetry? There are literally tens of thousands of poets writing in the United States today, and literally thousands and thousands of them publish, and not just in magazines, they publish volumes. Every day, literally, unsolicitedly, volumes of poetry, published and unpublished, reach me in the mail. It is a never-ending flow.'"

The answer to Hazlitt's and Bloom's questions is not that we want or need more culture, but that the evanescence of the third kind of meaning ensures that humans are forever trying, through participation in culture—at least so far as it is culture and not merely the sociology of culture—to recover meanings once glimpsed and now lost in the quotidian. "Poetry is the consolation of mortal men," writes Emerson: "They live cabined, cribbed, confined in a narrow and trivial lot,—in wants, pains, anxieties and superstitions, in personal animosities, in mean employments." Some seek poetry's consolations by composing poetry; others participate by appreciating and appropriating the poems of the great poets. For poetry, as Keats saw, "should strike the Reader as a wording of his own highest thoughts, and appear almost a remembrance." And yet even then the reality is not presence but absence. "The works of art & the works of nature," writes Emerson, "are all monuments on which some record is inscribed of departed strength & faded glory."

The human compulsion that leads to repetitions, along with the seriousness of the attempt to grasp or at least symbolize the evanescence experienced as meaning in itself, dictates the structure of cultural productivity. The special languages of the Kantian critiques, like those of the Platonic dialogues, both protect their witness to transcendent meaning and simultaneously render fealty to the accretions of the quotidian, where thought is almost entirely constituted by the lateral progression of translational activity. Emphasis after emphasis displaces itself into equivalence, and these discursive extensions swirl and eddy for vast distances around the very small core of transcendent meanings that cannot be made equivalent. To demonstrate in detail the subliminal drifting of one such extension, and at the same time to encapsulate before our very eyes a new shape of culture, will be the task of the ensuing discussion. It will, one hopes, seem to have as much interest as other cultural production can claim. In addition, to illustrate how rapidly cultural interconnections proliferate, and how intricate they quickly tend to become, though encapsulated in shapes, a special denseness of argument and reference will be aimed at. To that end specialist knowledge and general culture will be intertwined to weave a close texture of discourse in both this chapter and the concluding one.

The fact that almost all meanings are meanings by equivalence, conveyed by some form of translation, exerts a directional force on culture. Though cultural forms exist in the arena of history, and thus descend in chronological sequences that make their structure vertical, the translational pressure imparts a lateral tendency that tugs at the integrity of these forms. When enough such pressure accumulates, the forms break out of their linearity and stream across one another to become idiosyncratic shapes. Such a shape, evolving in laminated layers consisting of portions of several forms, occurs when analytical attention is directed to a particularly significant cultural node of meaning. This kind of shape can be illustrated by a consideration of the stream of meaning in Coleridge's well-known formula, "the willing suspension of disbelief."

Coleridge's prose is characteristically difficult to follow in any consecutive way, as was apparently true of his conversation as well; but in both prose and conversation brilliant statements paradoxically arise from the mists. Carlyle, in an unfriendly description, makes the point as well as anyone has (he is speaking of the last decade of Coleridge's life):

> Nothing could be more copious than his talk . . . not flowing anywhither like a river, but spreading everywhither in inextricable currents and regurgitations like a lake or sea. . . . So that, most times, you felt logically lost; swamped near to drowning in this tide of ingenious vocables, spreading out boundless as if to submerge the world . . . and you swam and fluttered in the mistiest wide unintelligible deluge of things. . . . Glorious islets, too, I have seen rise out of the haze. . . . Balmy sunny islets, islets of the blest and the intelligible:—on which occasions those secondary humming groups would all cease humming, and hang breathless upon the eloquent words; till once your islet got wrapt in the mist again, and they would recommence humming.

We all know many of those glorious islets. The two paragraphs at the end of chapter 13 of the *Biographia Literaria*, where Coleridge distinguishes primary imagination, secondary imagination, and fancy, may well be the most famous brief prose passage in all of English literature. A casual remark about Iago's statement of his reasons for hating Othello elicits a condensed description, "the motive-hunting of a motiveless malignity," which has reverberated through endless requoting by later critics. Other examples crowd to mind, but I wish to talk in this chapter about only one, the formulation, "the willing suspension of disbelief," which is perhaps as well known to intellectuals as any five words in the language.

The full statement, which occurs in the fourteenth chapter of *Biographia Literaria* and refers to Coleridge's part in the plan of *Lyrical Ballads*, runs this way:

> It was agreed, that my endeavours should be directed to persons and characters supernatural, or at least romantic; yet so as to transfer from our inward nature a human interest and a semblance of truth sufficient to procure for these shadows of imagination that willing suspension of disbelief for the moment, which constitutes poetic faith.

I shall attempt in this chapter to tease out certain strands in the texture of this statement to show that they associate with matters that do not appear on the surface. Though it may appear that I am thereby embarking on an orthodox Derridean deconstruction, I conceive myself as doing something analogous to that, or rather, partly analogous to that, instead of the thing itself. Doubtless it would not have occurred to me to discuss the passage in the way I shall without the astral influence, so to speak, of French theories of structuralism, intertextuality, and deconstruction. We are all aware of such theories, even if out of the corner of our eye, and they are exerting massive influence upon the way we approach literary texts. But deconstruction properly so called teases out strands that reveal an alogicality in the surface statement that eventually dismantles its intent, or, in Paul de Man's formulation, an authorial blindness that is the condition of authorial insight. Although I shall be dealing with matters subliminal to and eventually remote from the text at hand, I shall seek no alogical or conflicting elements, and therefore the process is not properly speaking one of deconstruction, but rather one of expansion. I am attempting to limn a shape of culture, not subvert my chosen text.

Besides, Coleridge himself, with his undying hostility to all things

French, excepting Descartes and Pascal, would be mortified to think that his remains were being dissected by French pathologists. He would feel himself in more sympathetic hands in the exclusively English tradition of Leavis, who tells us, in *The Common Pursuit:*

> The critic will be especially wary how he uses extraneous knowledge about the writer's intentions. Intentions are nothing in art except as realized, and the tests of realization will remain what they were. They are applied in the operation of the critic's sensibility; they are a matter of sense, derived from his literary experience, of what the living thing feels like—of the difference between that which has been willed and put there, or represents no profound integration, and that which grows from a deep centre of life. These tests may very well reveal that the deep animating intention (if that is the right word) is something very different from the intention the author would declare.

In these terms, I shall be seeking the "deep centre of life" from which Coleridge's statement grew. And as to my process itself, it might be called Empsonian rather than Derridean, for Empson might be described as a uniquely gifted structuralist without the characteristic structuralist system of reference. I shall in a way, indeed, consider "disbelief" as a "complex word" that becomes, in Empson's phrase, a "compacted doctrine."

I have emphasized with respect to my chosen text, "the willing suspension of disbelief," that it is very famous, supremely famous, if one wishes, and in a sense what I am saying constitutes an attempt to account for why that is so. But purely within the expectations of ordinary language, the fame of the passage conceals from us a fact that analytical attention immediately makes obvious: that is, that it is an unusual, even a peculiar statement. It is not what one would expect from the ordinary use of language or the normal demands of the seeming situation. It is the negative of a positive that has been suppressed. Instead of "suspension of disbelief for the moment," ordinary usage would suggest some such phrase as "temporary belief." With this substitution, the statement would run, not "that willing suspension of disbelief for the moment, which constitutes poetic faith," but rather "that temporary belief, which constitutes poetic faith." Certainly the only difference on the surface is that one would not ordinarily take the long way around with "suspension of disbelief for the moment," but would naturally refer to "temporary belief." On that level the two statements mean quite the same thing, except that the former would not normally be said.

The first possible qualification to such a contention is that perhaps Coleridge did not have any definite end in view but was, so to speak, just talking. Or to rephrase in Leavisian terms, the first qualification is that Coleridge perhaps did not make the statement in the context of his "deep animating intention." Since "suspension of disbelief for the moment" is acceptable English, with regard both to syntax and diction, the element of free play in any stream of discourse might well account for it as a simply random variation of the more probable and economical "temporary belief."

We must, however, rule out this possibility; for Coleridge, a few chapters later, again begins to talk about the nature of poetic faith, and he does so specifically in the matrix of a negative rendering of the act of belief; for he speaks of "that *illusion,* contra-distinguished from *delusion,* that negative faith, which simply permits the images presented to work by their own force, without either denial of or affirmation of their real existence by the judgment." The negative context here is so specific that it no doubt brings to our mind what Keats called the "quality" that "went to form a Man of Achievement especially in Literature & which Shakespeare possessed so enormously—I mean *Negative Capability,* that is when man is capable of being in uncertainties, Mysteries, doubts, without any irritable reaching after fact & reason." Keats was here writing in late December of the same year, 1817, in which the *Biographia Literaria* was published, and the possible connection with Coleridge is made more challenging by his immediately following specification: "Coleridge, for instance, would let go by a fine isolated verisimilitude caught from the Penetralium of mystery, from being incapable of remaining content with half knowledge." If we were following a deconstructive trail to Keats himself, we would note that Coleridge, of all people, does not answer to the charge and that Keats, in his concluding question in the "Ode to a Nightingale," "Do I wake or sleep?" precisely does. We could note the precedence of Wordsworth's "wise passiveness" to the formulations of both Coleridge and Keats. And we could also note Sidney Colvin's comment on "Penetralium of mystery": "An admirable phrase!—if only *penetralium* were Latin."

I do not wish on this occasion, however, to pursue such indications of turmoil and alogicality in Keats's formulation, but rather simply to bring it forward to buttress the intended negativity of Coleridge's choice of "suspension of disbelief." If further buttressing is needed, we can find it in Coleridge's correspondence in 1816, the same period when the *Biographia* was being produced:

> Images and Thoughts possess a power in and of themselves, independent of that act of the Judgment or Understanding by which we affirm or deny the existence of a reality correspondent to them. Such is the ordinary state of the mind in *Dreams*. It is not strictly accurate to say, that we believe our dreams to be actual while we are dreaming. We neither believe it or disbelieve it—with the will the comparing power is suspended, and without the comparing power any act of Judgment, whether affirmation or denial, is impossible.

The same kind of emphasis obtains in his comments on dramatic illusion, where he says that it is a "mistaken opinion, that in our *ordinary* dreams we judge the objects to be real." What "pictures are to little children, stage-illusion is to men," except that "in the latter instance this suspension of the act of comparison, which permits this sort of negative belief, is somewhat more assisted by the will than in that of the child respecting a picture." "These and all other stage presentations . . . produce a sort of temporary half-faith, which the spectator encourages in himself and supports by a voluntary contribution on his own part, because he knows that it is at all times in his power to see the thing as it really is." Here the invocation of "suspension," of "will," of "negative belief," as well as the explanation surrounding "temporary half-faith," all support the premise that the choice of words in "willing suspension of disbelief" is deliberate and precise rather than adventitious.

So the special phrasing, "suspension of disbelief," must be accepted as issuing from Coleridge's "deep animating intention." It is thus an idiosyncratic entry for a perennial debate in literary criticism and theory. For instance, the English Institute Essays for 1957 bear the title *Literature and Belief,* while the final chapter of I. A. Richards's *Principles of Literary Criticism* in 1924 is called "Poetry and Beliefs." Such discussions cannot of course have been in Coleridge's mind, but the arguments of their authors are presumably accessible at all periods, and at any rate Coleridge was very much in *their* minds. In the English Institute volume is a contribution by M. H. Abrams called "Belief and the Willing Suspension of Disbelief," while Richards for his part says that

> Coleridge, when he remarked that "a willing suspension of disbelief" accompanied much poetry, was noting an important fact, but not quite in the happiest terms, for we are neither aware of a disbelief nor voluntarily suspending it in these cases. It is better to say that the question of belief or disbelief, in the intellectual sense, never arises when we are reading well.

Richards's proviso seems reasonable, and it is in fact precisely what Coleridge himself has said in the letter quoted above: Richards argues that "the question of belief or disbelief . . . never arises," and Coleridge confirms that "we neither believe it or disbelieve it." Coleridge, we remember, is referring to dreams, but the connection between poem and dream was close for any good Romantic, and in fact Coleridge's own "Kubla Khan" is subtitled "A Vision in a Dream." The joint effect of Coleridge's comment in his letter and of Richards's objection is to reinforce the sense that "the willing suspension of disbelief" differs from the language of ordinary expectation.

The statement of Richards's just brought forward is from his *Practical Criticism* of 1929 rather than from his *Principles of Literary Criticism* of 1924, and it shows the problem of poetry and belief to be of continuing urgency in his thought. In fact, in the later work he says early on, "It is plain that the doctrinal problem, the place and importance of beliefs in poetry, is in need of discussion," and in a subsequent chapter he discusses the topic with reference specifically to religion and poetry. He there says of Donne's sonnet about the day of resurrection, "It becomes very difficult not to think that *actual belief* in the doctrine that appears in the poem is required for its full and perfect imaginative realisation." His "protocol" experiments with student readers led him to conclude "that many who try to read religious poetry find themselves strongly invited to the beliefs presented, and that doctrinal dissent is a very serious obstacle to their reading. Conversely, many successful but dissenting readers find themselves in a mental attitude towards the doctrine which, if it is not belief, closely resembles belief."

This thesis generated an immediate antithesis. In his long essay on Dante, published later in the same year (1929) as *Practical Criticism*, T. S. Eliot found the problem of belief central to a reading of the *Divine Comedy* and took extended issue with Richards. Arguing that "the question of what Dante 'believed' is always relevant," Eliot then offers a discrimination:

> My point is that you cannot afford to *ignore* Dante's philosophical and theological beliefs, or to skip the passages which express them most clearly; but that on the other hand you are not called upon to believe them yourself. It is wrong to think that there are parts of the *Divine Comedy* which are of interest only to Catholics or to mediaevalists. For there is a difference (which here I hardly do more than assert) between philosophical *belief* and poetic *assent*.

If this sounds like a covert restatement of Coleridge's position, with "poetic assent" standing in for "willing suspension of disbelief," our sense of the fact is reinforced when Eliot shortly afterwards says that "if you can read poetry as poetry, you will 'believe' in Dante's theology exactly as you believe in the physical reality of his journey; that is, you suspend both belief and disbelief."

In all three of these modern usages—those of Eliot, Richards, and Abrams—Coleridge's "suspension of disbelief" forces, as it were, its special formulation into the din of argument and thus echoes back to its original matrix with renewed plangency. The peculiarity of his phrasing notwithstanding, Coleridge has clearly sounded a theme that reverberates centrally in literary theory.

That it does so reverberate, I shall argue, is the result of polyphonic doublings by hidden instruments, those of philosophy and theology. Perhaps no figure in all of literature—or perhaps I should say, because of the extraordinary disarray of Coleridge's production, in all of *écriture*—presents texts more seemingly fragmentary but actually more complexly interconnected than does Coleridge. As L. C. Knights has said, "In Coleridge, everything is connected to everything else." Hazlitt, writing with a wonderful mixture of admiration and hostility, speaks almost despairingly of Coleridge as

> the man of perhaps the greatest ability now living . . . who has not only done the least, but who is actually incapable of ever doing any thing worthy of him—unless he had a hundred hands to write with, and a hundred mouths to utter all that it hath entered into his heart to conceive, and centuries before him to embody the endless volume of his waking dreams. Cloud rolls over cloud; one train of thought suggests and is driven away by another; theory after theory is spun out of the bowels of his brain. . . . No subject can come amiss to him . . . his mind every where finding its level, and feeling no limit but that of thought . . . passing from Duns Scotus to Jacob Behmen, from the Kantean philosophy to a conundrum, and from the Apocalypse to an acrostic—taking in the whole range of poetry, painting, wit, history, politics, metaphysics, criticism, and private scandal—every question giving birth to some new thought, and every thought "discoursed in eloquent music," that lives only in the ear of fools, or in the report of absent friends. Set him to write a book, and he belies all that has been ever said about him—
>   "Ten thousand great ideas filled his mind,
>   But with the clouds they fled, and left no trace behind."

This judgment notwithstanding, traces of many things can be found in abundance in Coleridge, as Hazlitt's description of the flowing together of his topics might suggest. Indeed, though we are beguiled by the wit of Carlyle's metaphor of the stream of Coleridge's conversation spreading out into a sea from which rise glorious islets of intelligibility, a truer metaphor might be that of a lava flow, which congeals at points into the glorious islets; for Carlyle's usage sets the islets in opposition to the flow, as being of different substance, whereas the ineluctable truth is that the islets and the flow are of the same substance. De Quincey, in his account of his first meeting with Coleridge, provides memorable formulation for this truth:

> Coleridge led me to a drawing-room, rang the bell for refreshments, and omitted no point of a courteous reception. . . . And these little points of business being settled,—Coleridge, like some great river, the Orellana, or the St Lawrence, that had been checked and fretted by rocks or thwarting islands, and suddenly recovers its volume of waters, and its mighty music— swept at once, as if returning to his natural business, into a continuous strain of eloquent dissertation, certainly the most novel, and traversing the most spacious fields of thought, by transitions the most just and logical, that it was possible to conceive. What I mean by saying that his transitions were "just," is by way of contradistinction to that mode of conversation which courts variety by means of *verbal* connections. Coleridge, to many people, and often I have heard the complaint, seemed to wander; and he seemed then to wander the most, when in fact his resistance to the wandering instinct was greatest,—viz. when the compass, and huge circuit, by which his illustrations moved, travelled farthest into remote regions, before they began to revolve. Long before this coming round commenced, most people had lost him, and naturally enough supposed he had lost himself. They continued to admire the separate beauty of his thoughts, but did not see their relations to the dominant theme.

De Quincey goes on to stress the logic that underlies Coleridge's multitudinous ideas: "I can assert," he says, "upon my long and intimate knowledge of Coleridge's mind, that logic, the most severe, was as inalienable from his modes of thinking, as grammar from his language."

If we accept this sort of firsthand testimony to the extended range and logical interconnection of Coleridge's discourse, it may seem reasonable to suspect that "the willing suspension of disbelief" is not only a separate beauty or islet, but also relates to a dominant theme that extends into regions remote from our immediate purview.

The doorway to these regions may swing open if we find its hidden hinge. That hinge, I urge, is the word *disbelief*, and the pressure needed to unlatch the doorway should be applied to the question of why Coleridge says disbelief rather than belief or some other positive, such as Eliot's "poetic *assent.*"

If we put a string or elastic through a playing card, hold the ends in our hands, and tighten the string by moving our hands apart, the card will tend to turn over. The double force produces a kind of torque, and by this crude analogy I shall attempt to account for the expected word *belief* turning over into *disbelief.* In the chronological as well as syntactical linearity of the context of "suspension of disbelief," we find the kind of double traction that might generate the torque we seek. Coleridge's passage, as we have seen, relates forward in time to twentieth-century statement, statement of a certain kind that we call poetic theory. It relates backward in time, however, to another kind of statement that we call philosophical. The oppositions implicit in these two kinds generate the first moment of the required torque.

Indeed, the paradigm for this kind of torque may be found in Plato's phrase, at *Republic* 607B, about the *palaia diaphora*, or ancient quarrel, between poetry and philosophy. Plato, as we will remember, excludes poets from his ideal commonwealth on the grounds that they are liars, that is, that they cannot be believed. What, then, is the proper object of belief? Simply that which is true. But mimetic poets, as Plato says at *Republic* 603A, are "makers of images far removed from the truth."

Belief, however, though related to truth, is related only contingently. The mental act that is related necessarily to truth is knowledge. Belief, indeed, may be defined as hypothetical knowledge of truth, or conversely, as knowledge of hypothetical truth. Belief is thus a lower-order function, knowledge a higher-order function, in the same vector of attention. We see this in compressed form in Augustine's "credo ut intelligam"—"I believe that I may know." Again, Plato, in his discussion of the four stages of intelligence in books 6 and 7 of *The Republic*, sets up the famous proportion by which *eikasia*, or imaginative conjecture, relates to *pistis*, or belief, in the same way that *dianoia*, that is, understanding, relates to *epis-*

tēmē, the highest state in the general field of *gnōsis*, or knowledge. *Pistis*, or belief, is thus preliminary to knowledge.

But we may well ask, if knowledge is superior to belief—and belief gives way to knowledge—why do we not simply jettison belief and concentrate all our efforts on knowledge? The answer is that the structure of the human mind makes belief a necessary function. All human experience is founded on the category of possibility, which is divided from actuality by the subjunction *might*. It is this truth that dictates Karl Jaspers's definition of human life as *mögliche Existenz*, possible existence. In God, however, who is theologically defined as *actus purus*, there could be no possibility, because all possibility would be identical with actuality. Possibility is the measure of our limitation, and it is only for limited human intelligence that something may or may not be, that something be done or not be done. I might go to the market, or I might not. Only when I do go does the *might* disappear into actuality.

Thus Kant distinguishes between a hypothetical *intellectus archetypus* and our own minds, which are *intellectus ectypus*. The former would be "an understanding that, not being discursive like ours, but intuitive, proceeds from the *synthetic universal*, or intuition of a whole as a whole, to the particular, that is to say, from the whole to the parts. . . . Our own understanding, on the contrary, must advance from the parts . . . to different possible forms." Kant goes on to say that "it is not necessary to prove that such an *intellectus archetypus* is possible. It is sufficient to show that we are led to this idea of an *intellectus archetypus* by contrasting with it our discursive understanding that has need of images (*intellectus ectypus*) and noting the contingent character of such an *intellectus ectypus*, and that the idea of the *intellectus archetypus* involves nothing contradictory." In other words, *intellectus archetypus* would be an understanding that knows only reality, and *intellectus ectypus* is the one we actually possess, which knows actuality only as contrasted to possibility. *Intellectus ectypus*, we immediately realize, is similar to Plato's doxic proportion of *eikasia* and *pistis*, for it is characterized by that bonding of possibility and actuality which accounts for belief, and it also needs images in the manner of *eikasia*.

The distinction of the two kinds of understanding comes at an extraordinarily important locus in Kant. Schelling said of the progression of argument culminating here that perhaps never before had so many profound thoughts been crammed into so few pages. Cassirer, in our own day, says for his part that "all the lines previously established by the critique of reason here converge in a single point. . . . The inquiry here passes into depths which are genuine and ultimate, into the very foundations of the Kantian conceptual structure."

At this juncture, before we proceed to load still more philosophical weight onto the antecedence of "willing suspension of disbelief," perhaps it is well to take heed of the possible disbelief of my readers that such antecedence is relevant. After all, is not Coleridge writing about the purpose of his own poetry in a book specifically subtitled *Biographical Sketches of My Literary Life and Opinions?* Indeed he is. But he had been thinking about the *Biographia Literaria* for some fifteen years before he got around to writing it. Perhaps his earliest reference to the treatise can be traced back to 1800, where he lists the "works which I gird myself up to attack as soon as money concerns will permit" as including "the Life of Lessing—& the Essay on Poetry. The latter is still more at my heart than the former—its Title would be an Essay on the Elements of Poetry / it would in reality be a *disguised* System of Morals & Politics." So from the very outset, Coleridge intended his statement about poetic matters to ramify into larger concerns. By 1801 the philosophical tropism is even more pronounced, for he says:

> Let me work as hard as I can, I shall not be able to do what my heart within me *burns* to do—that is, *concenter* my free mind to the affinities of the Feelings with Words & Ideas under the title of "Concerning Poetry & the nature of the Pleasures derived from it."—I have faith, that I do understand this subject / and I am sure, that if I write what I ought to do on it, the Work would supersede all the Books of Metaphysics hitherto written / and all the Books of Morals too.

When the *Biographia Literaria* actually appeared in 1817, therefore, it quite fittingly said on its very first page that its narrative was to be "introductory to the statement of my principles in Politics, Religion, and Philosophy, and an application of the rules, deduced from philosophical principles, to poetry and criticism." We are therefore certainly not straining the situation to adduce philosophical antecedents for Coleridge's literary-theoretical statement. Nor are we straining matters to locate those antecedents in Plato and Kant. "Of all the knowledge with which Coleridge worked," observes I. A. Richards, "none went deeper or did more than what he had learned from Plato." After all, as Coleridge says in chapter 12 of the *Biographia,* his system scientifically arranged would be "according to my conviction, no other than the system of Pythagoras and Plato revived and purified from impure mixtures." And as to Kant, Coleridge notes in chapter 9 of the *Biographia:*

The writings of the illustrious sage of Königsberg, the founder of the Critical Philosophy, more than any other work, at once invigorated and disciplined my understanding. The originality, the depth, and the compression of the thoughts; the novelty and subtlety, yet solidity and importance of the distinctions; the adamantine chain of the logic; and I will venture to add (paradox as it will appear to those who have taken their notion of IMMANUEL KANT from Reviewers and Frenchmen) the *clearness* and *evidence,* of the "CRITIQUE OF THE PURE REASON"; of the JUDGEMENT; of the "METAPHISICAL ELEMENTS OF NATURAL PHILOSOPHY," and of his "RELIGION WITHIN THE BOUNDS OF PURE REASON," took possession of me with a giant's hand. After fifteen years familiarity with them, I still read these and all his other productions with undiminished delight and increasing admiration.

The *Kritik der Urteilskraft,* or *Critique of Judgment,* which is where Kant's distinction of *intellectus archetypus* and *intellectus ectypus* appears, was a special object of Coleridge's admiration. "Of Kant C[oleridge] spoke in terms of high admiration . . ." records Henry Crabb Robinson in 1810. "His *Critik der Urtheilskraft* he considered as the most astonishing of his works."

So the philosophical thought of Plato and Kant might reasonably seem to exert a massive pull against the literary-theoretical descendance of "willing suspension of disbelief." A second moment of opposing pressure, augmenting these forces that generate traction in the chronological line, is supplied by the syntactic matrix of "suspension of disbelief." Adjacent to this phrase, and indeed framing it, are two words that contain a truly enormous dynamic charge in Coleridge's vocabulary: the first is *imagination* and the second *faith.* One comes before and one comes after: "to procure for these shadows of imagination that willing suspension of disbelief for the moment, which constitutes poetic faith."

We need little citation to document the importance of imagination in Coleridge's theoretical commitment, especially when talking of the *Biographia Literaria.* The imagination nominated in the sentence about the "suspension of disbelief" occurs, indeed, at the beginning of the fourteenth chapter, only a few paragraphs after Coleridge, at the end of the thirteenth chapter, has propounded his threefold distinction of primary imagination, secondary imagination, and fancy. The explication of the functions of the imaginative faculties, furthermore, has been a declared object of the work as a whole.

Charged though *imagination* is in Coleridge's scheme of things, however, not even that word can match the monumental centrality of the word *faith.* It is no exaggeration to say that the consuming purpose of Coleridge's life as he saw it was a defense of the Christian faith. One of the titles proposed for his fabled magnum opus sums it all up: *Christianity the One True Philosophy.* As he says in 1816, "To recommend that state of mind, which looks forward to the 'fellowship of the mystery of the faith as a spirit of wisdom and revelation in the KNOWLEDGE of God, the eyes of the UNDERSTANDING being enlightened'—this formed my GENERAL purpose." He continues: "Long has it been at my heart! I consider it as the contradistinguishing principle of Christianity that in it alone . . . the Understanding . . . culminates in Faith, as its crown of Glory."

Faith, indeed, might well be described as a word that in Coleridge functions as what Empson calls a "master symbol," which is present when "the doctrine of the author is felt to be absorbed into his whole style, and particularly present in the style when he uses this key word." Certainly the faith in God that constitutes the center of Christianity was for Coleridge the comprehensive idea, the umbrella, so to speak, under which all his various endeavors ranged themselves. "I can truly affirm of myself," he writes in 1816, "that my studies have been profitable and availing to me only so far, as I have endeavoured to use all my other knowledge as a glass enabling me to receive more light in a wider field of vision from the word of God." The "willing suspension of disbelief for the moment, which constitutes poetic faith" must first of all be recognized in this context; it stands in the "light of a wider field of vision from the word of God."

The situation here is the same as that with one of Coleridge's best-known literary-theoretical formulations, the distinction between symbol and allegory. Or rather, the formulation is literary-theoretical to us, but theological to Coleridge; it stands directly under the umbrella of faith. The definition as Coleridge gives it runs this way:

> Now an Allegory is but a translation of abstract notions into a picture-language which is itself nothing but an abstraction from objects of the senses; the principle being more worthless even than its phantom proxy, both alike unsubstantial, and the former shapeless to boot. On the other hand a Symbol . . . is characterized by a translucence of the Special in the Individual or of the General in the Especial or of the Universal in the General. Above all by the translucence of the Eternal through and in the Temporal. It always partakes of the Reality which it renders intelligible; and while it enunciates the whole, abides itself as a living part in that Unity of which it is the representative.

We are so used to admiring this passage out of context that we often are not aware of what immediately precedes the distinction: "It is among the miseries of the present age that it recognizes no medium between *Literal* and *Metaphorical*. Faith is either to be buried in the dead letter, or its name and honors usurped by a counterfeit product of the mechanical understanding, which in the blindness of self-complacency confounds SYMBOLS with ALLEGORIES."

If the distinction between symbol and allegory relates directly to faith, so, and even more directly, does the "willing suspension of disbelief." In Greek, the word *pistis* means both "belief" and "faith," and almost all the ancient declarations of Christian faith, as we can see by consulting J. N. D. Kelly's *Early Christian Creeds,* begin with the words "I believe," or, if reflecting their origin in a synod, "we believe," that is, in Greek with a *pisteuō* or *pisteuomen* and in Latin with a *credo* or *credimus.* So a typical formula might run "Pisteuomen eis hena theon" and conclude with an asseveration of belief in the Holy Spirit as well, or do the same from a Latin beginning such as "Credo in unum deum" or "Credo in deum patrem omnipotentem."

Though declarations of faith begin with a statement of belief, Coleridge, utilizing the distinction of the two words in English, argues that faith and belief are not the same. He warns against confounding "the act of faith with the assent of the fancy and understanding to certain words and conceptions," and against "a confusion of faith with belief." "Faith," on the contrary, is, as he says "the *apotheosis* of the reason in man, the complement of reason, the will in the form of reason." "Faith," again, "seems to me the co-adunation of the individual will with the reason, enforcing adherence alike of thought, act, and affection to the Universal Will, whether revealed in the conscience, or by the light of reason." Or, "FAITH may be defined, as fidelity to our own being." In another sense, "faith is fidelity, fealty, allegiance of the moral nature to God"; "faith is properly a state and disposition of the will, or rather of the whole man, the I." And finally:

> Faith subsists in the *synthesis* of the reason and the individual will. By virtue of the latter therefore it must be an energy, and inasmuch as it relates to the whole moral man, it must be exerted in each and all of his constituents or incidents, faculties and tendencies:—it must be a total, not a partial; a continuous, not a desultory or occasional energy. And by virtue of the former, that is, reason, faith must be a light, a form of knowing, a beholding of truth.

In such contexts, it is apparent why faith cannot be equated with belief considered as simple assent, and Coleridge dramatizes the contrast by the neat logical point that the devils believe, though they do not have faith. Speaking of "the practical mischiefs resulting from the confusion of Belief and Faith," he says:

> Yet how early the dangerous identification of the two words began, we learn from the Epistle of James, who, arguing *ex absurdo* on the assumption, that Faith means Belief, justly remarks—The Devils believe, and so thoroughly too, that they believe and tremble. Belief, therefore, can not be the proper and essential ground of Salvation in the soul. But Faith *is,* and by Christ himself is solemnly declared to be so. Therefore, Belief can not be the same as Faith! though the Belief of the truths essential to the Faith in Christ is the necessary accompaniment and consequent of the Faith.

This breaking apart or desynonymizing of faith and belief tends, analogically speaking, to exert force from the stronger entity, faith, against the weaker, belief. The torque is made more definite by a twist given to faith. For the faith nominated in the syntactic environs of "suspension of disbelief" is turned from its larger function into a partial negative: it is not faith as such, but "poetic faith." As Coleridge says in chapter 22 of the *Biographia,* about the negative faith that is another name for "the willing suspension of disbelief," "A faith, which transcends even historic belief, must absolutely *put out* this mere poetic Analogon of faith as the summer sun is said to extinguish our household fires, when it shines full upon them. What would otherwise have been yielded to as pleasing fiction, is repelled as revolting falsehood." So poetic faith is here more specifically denominated "this mere poetic Analogon of faith."

Kant tells us why. "*Cognisable* things are of three kinds," he says: "*things of opinion (opinionabile); things of fact (scibile);* and *things of faith (mere credibile).*" Of this last he says, "the Being of God and the immortality of the soul are *things of faith (res fidei),* and of all objects are the only ones that can be so called." Coleridge's concern for philosophical precision therefore makes it necessary when he invokes his master symbol, faith, to distinguish the usage here from the only proper reference of the word by the diminishing adjective *poetic*, which also echoes Plato's rejection of poets as liars.

A similar situation obtains with the other key word, *imagination*, which stands in the immediately prior syntactic environs of "willing suspension of disbelief." For here, just as *faith* is twisted from its positive into the partial negative of "poetic faith," so *imagination* is twisted into "shadows of imagination." We can see how sharp the twist is by reminding ourselves that, just three paragraphs before, "primary imagination" has been lauded as "the living Power and prime Agent of all human Perception, and as a repetition in the finite mind of the eternal act of creation in the infinite I AM," while "secondary imagination" has been honored as "identical with the primary in the *kind* of its agency, and differing only in *degree*, and in the *mode* of its operation." This honorific status, the Platonic lineage of which in Coleridge's mind can be traced at least as far back as Ficino's *Platonica Theologia*, now gives way to "shadows of imagination."

"The Living Power and prime Agent of all human Perception" is thus reduced to "shadows of imagination," which is to say that an emphasis in the tradition of Plato is eclipsed by an emphasis in Plato himself. For "shadows of imagination" would be an excellent translation for *eikasia*, which is the lowest of the four states of intelligence in Plato's scheme. As R. L. Nettleship observes in his respected *Lectures on the Republic of Plato:*

> The literal translation of *eikasia* is "imagination." But it would be very misleading to translate the one word by the other; for, while *eikasia* expresses the superficial side of what we call imagination, it does not express the deeper side. Imagination in English has two senses. In one sense it really does answer to Plato's conception of seeing images. When we say that something is a mere imagination, or that a man is the slave of his own imagination, we do mean to describe a very superficial view of things.

The other sense of imagination, of course, is the one hypostatized by Coleridge's honorific formulas for primary and secondary imagination. But in the present instance Coleridge is talking of something that corresponds to Plato's specific usage, *eikasia*, which must be rendered not as "imagination" but as "shadows of imagination." A collage of quotations from Nettleship will elucidate the point:

> The most superficial view of the world, that which conveys least knowledge of it, is called by Plato *eikasia*. . . . The mental state is one of the very little certitude, its objects are of the nature of "images," shadows and reflexions.
>
> Why does he describe this lowest group of objects as shadows or reflexions? Shadows, images and dreams, are the most obvious types of unreality, and the contrast between them and realities is very striking to early thinkers. . . .

Nettleship sums up in a way that guarantees the propriety of Coleridge's "shadows of imagination": "Any state of mind of which the object stands to some other object as a shadow or reflexion does to the real thing, is *eikasia*."

But Nettleship emphasizes that "the moment a man knows that a shadow is only a shadow, or a picture only a picture, he is no longer in a state of *eikasia* in that particular respect." This seems precisely Coleridge's point in identifying the poetic function as "shadows of imagination": he invokes *eikasia* to free himself from it. As Nettleship observes:

> We are all in a state of *eikasia* about many things, and to get a general idea of the sort of views that Plato had in mind when he spoke of shadows and reflexions which are taken for realities we must think how many views there are which circulate in society and form a large part of what we call knowledge, but which when we examine them are seen to be distorted, imperfect representations of fact.

In other words, Coleridge is saying in the intertext of his passage what Plato says at *Republic* 608A: "We must not take such poetry seriously as a serious thing that lays hold on truth." Though a great poet himself, Coleridge is insisting that in any final systematic accounting, poetry is an *eikasia*, is merely a shadow of knowledge, a "distorted, imperfect representation of fact." That his statement here wholly reflects the Platonic analysis may be confirmed by considering the key word immediately prior to *imagination,* which is *truth:* "a semblance of truth sufficient to procure for these shadows of imagination that willing suspension of disbelief for the moment, which constitutes poetic faith." *Truth,* in the Platonic analysis, is an ultimate word; it is, as Plato says at *Republic* 508D–E, coordinate with *reality (alētheia te kai to on)* and with *knowledge (epistēmēn de kai alētheian).*

So we have in alignment four nouns, key words each: *truth, imagination, belief,* and *faith;* and we have controlling them the participle *willing,* which for Coleridge represents a fifth noun that in a progression from *The Friend* through *Aids to Reflection* became the most important word of all. "The free will," he says even in the *Biographia,* "is our only absolute self." Accordingly, *will* in participial form controls the four nouns, which are turned to equivocal significances: *truth* is twisted to "semblance of truth," *imagination* to "shadows of imagination," *belief* to "disbelief," *faith* to "poetic faith."

The four words tend to group themselves into pairs. *Truth* and *imagination* are joined by Platonic reference, *belief* and *faith* by Christian reference. With poetry as the subject of discourse, the weight of Platonic concerns twists the first two, and the weight of Christian concerns the latter pair. That the double weight of these concerns is sufficient may be inferred from Coleridge's testimony that "if there be any two subjects which have in the very depth of my Nature interested me, it has been the Hebrew & Christian Theology, & the Theology of Plato."

Kant, too, contributes to the torque. Indeed, the whole turning process by which the four words are readjusted into their equivocal significances might be described as changing their ideal reference from the conception of *intellectus archetypus* to that of *intellectus ectypus:* for *intellectus ectypus,* which divides reality from possibility, generates those feignings and fictions of poetry that in ultimate contexts can be stigmatized as false knowledge. Near the end of the *Critique of Pure Reason* Kant asserts that all the interests of reason combine in three questions: "1. What can I know? 2. What ought I to do? 3. What may I hope?" There then follows a section in which he says that "the holding of a thing to be true, or the subjective validity of the judgment, in its relation to conviction . . . has the following three degrees: *opining* (*meinen*), *believing* (*glauben*), and *knowing* (*wissen*)." He defines all three in terms of the relationship of subject to object: "If our holding of a judgment be only subjectively sufficient, and is at the same time taken as being objectively insufficient, we have what is termed *believing*. . . . When the holding of a thing to be true is sufficient both subjectively and objectively, it is *knowledge*."

In the context of these elucidations, we can see that the Platonic *epistēmē*, which is coordinate with *truth*, would not be simply the knowledge of Kant's "What can I know?" but would be the answer to all three questions: "What can I know? What ought I to do? What may I hope?" Likewise, Christian faith could be described as the answer to the same three questions. It is deferred knowledge, but then so too is *alētheia*. The Bible, in the definition at Hebrews 11, says that "faith is the substance of things hoped for, the evidence of things not seen"; and Paul, in 1 Corinthians 13, coordinates faith and hope as symbols of knowledge, saying that "we know in part. . . . But when that which is perfect is come, that which is in part shall be done away with. . . . For now we see through a glass darkly; but then face to face: now I know in part; but then shall I know even as also I am known." Thus the progression from Kant's definition of believing as a subjectively sufficient holding and of knowing as a holding that is both subjectively and objectively sufficient subsumes the progression of Christian belief to Christian knowledge as well as that from Platonic belief to Platonic knowledge. Both lines of thought converge in Coleridge's insistence that "faith must be a light, a form of knowing, a beholding of truth"—a light, not the shadows of imagination; a form of knowing, not the conjectures of belief; a beholding of truth, not the semblance of truth.

One must not suppose, however, that Coleridge's qualifications in the "suspension of disbelief" passage mean that he was opposed to poetry as such. It is rather that in an ultimate accounting, which by its nature is something not often summoned, poetry must be seen to be only shadow and semblance, not the true object of faith.

Actually, there is culturally a kind of trompe l'oeil, as though a structure seen as concave were also, when gazed at steadily, revealed as convex; that is to say, *intellectus archetypus* is superior to *intellectus ectypus*, but the inferior understanding alone provides us the idea of the higher formation—much as the overwhelming grandeur of Shelley's Mont Blanc requires the puny awareness of human beings for its understanding. *Intellectus archetypus*, in brief, is paradoxically the creation of *intellectus ectypus*. Accordingly, though "the willing suspension of disbelief" emphasizes the concavity of the cultural shape, in other places Coleridge joins a great tradition of hailing its convexity, as when, in the very same chapter of the *Biographia*, he says that "the poet, described in *ideal* perfection, brings the whole soul of man into activity." This is the tradition of the great defenses of poetry by Sidney and by Shelley; it is the tradition in which Wordsworth can say that "to be incapable of a feeling of Poetry in my sense of the word is to be without love of human nature and reverence for God."

Nevertheless, though in such convexities poetry is seen as an adjunct of the ultimate (Wordsworth speaks of "the affinity between religion and poetry; between religion—making up the deficiencies of reason by faith; and poetry—passionate for the instruction of reason"), in the concavities of *intellectus archetypus* it must give way to still deeper concerns. For Coleridge, such concerns always were alpha and omega. Indeed, in the very last paragraph of the *Biographia* they assert their hegemony. "This has been my Object, and this alone can be my Defence . . ." says Coleridge there, "to kindle young minds, and to guard them against the temptations of Scorners, by showing that the Scheme of Christianity . . . though not discoverable by human Reason, is yet in accordance with it; that link follows link by necessary consequence; that Religion passes out of the ken of Reason only where the eye of Reason has reached its own Horizon; and that Faith is then but its continuation." For Coleridge the meanings of Christianity, and of its propaedeutic philosophers, Plato and Kant, took absolute precedence over the concerns of literary art even in that art's highest dignity.

But though the triple force of Plato, Kant, and Christianity accounts for the turning of the key words—*truth, imagination, belief, and faith*—there would seem to be still another force at work. There seems to be a perturbation in the torque. If only these three forces were there, we should expect belief to turn, but not to turn to *disbelief*. The expected turn would rather be to *unbelief;* for unbelief is the negative form of being as applied to faith: "Lord, I believe; help thou mine unbelief," runs the statement at Mark 9. "For what if some did not believe? shall their unbelief make the faith of God without effect?" is the question at Romans 3. This is the language of England in the early seventeenth century, as set forth in the King James version of the Bible. It was still the English language in Coleridge's day, as we may gauge by Hazlitt's statement concerning Shelley's atheism: "With all his faults, Mr. Shelley was an honest man. His unbelief and his presumption were parts of a disease, which was not combined in him either with indifference to human happiness, or contempt for human infirmities." Coleridge himself, elsewhere in the *Biographia Literaria,* says of the time when he almost lost his religious faith that he had skirted "the sandy deserts of utter unbelief."

Though *disbelief* and *unbelief* can often be roughly used as synonyms, when more precision is desired we sense a difference in their meanings. *Unbelief* seems to refer to a settled state that entails an entire position—as in Shelley's unbelief or Coleridge's "utter unbelief." *Disbelief,* on the other hand, seems to refer to something more fleeting and particular, to an attitude rather than to a position, as in "an expression of disbelief crossed his countenance." *Disbelief,* in short, tends to be coordinate with an attitude of skepticism, not with a settled denial.

Now, in Coleridge's day and even perhaps still in our own, attitudes of skepticism were associated more with the philosopher Hume than with any other figure; and it is the phantom hand of Hume, I shall suggest, that is also on the turning process, perturbing it slightly from a true rotation. I say phantom hand, for while Plato, Kant, and Christian apologists are highly visible and honored in Coleridge's background, Hume seems almost invisible. But he is very much there, even if in the manner noted by Empson's comment on the Keatsian line "No, no, go not to Lethe, neither twist," where he observes that "somebody, or some force in the poet's mind, must have wanted to go to Lethe very much, if it took four negatives in the first line to stop them." Both Empson's *mot* and Hume's absence from Coleridge's pantheon are examples of Alexander Gerard's third mode by which the imagination associates ideas: the first two are by way of resemblance and vicinity, but the third is by way of contrariety.

It is contrariety that keeps Hume relevant to Coleridge even while he is constantly being pushed into the background. Indeed, he is a fortiori the "Scorner" whose temptations Coleridge wishes to guard young minds against. Hume was the arch-enemy. "In digressing, in dilating, in passing from subject to subject, he appeared to me to float in air, to slide on ice," records Hazlitt of his first meeting with Coleridge in 1798: "He spoke slightingly of Hume (whose Essay on Miracles he said was stolen from an objection started in one of South's sermons . . .). I was not very much pleased at this account of Hume, for I had just been reading, with infinite relish, that completest of all metaphysical *choke-pears,* his *Treatise on Human Nature.* . . . Coleridge even denied the excellence of Hume's general style." For a single additional example, of a projected "History of Metaphysics in England from Lord Bacon to Mr. Hume," Coleridge writes in 1803 that "I confine myself to facts in every part of the work, excepting that which treats of Mr. Hume—*him* I have assuredly besprinkled copiously from the fountains of Bitterness and Contempt." Moreover, whenever Coleridge mentions Hume in the *Biographia* it is with disparagement, and in chapter 12 he gives the general reason for this rejection, by reference to "the impious and pernicious tenets defended by Hume, Priestley, and the French fatalists or necessitarians."

These tenets were simply those conceptions that tended to undermine Christian faith. Coleridge accordingly, in speaking in his first *Lay Sermon* in 1816 of Hume's history of England, nominates Hume as "the same Scotch philosopher, who devoted his life to the undermining of the Christian religion." To turn to the conclusion of the essay on miracles in the *Enquiries Concerning the Human Understanding,* which was the subject of Coleridge's initial disparagement recorded by Hazlitt, we find ample justification for the description of Hume as underminer. The passage is of course very famous, and is a touchstone for the rhetorical presentation of a state of unbelief through an attitude of disbelief. Hume concludes that the *Christian Religion* not only was at first attended with miracles, but even at this day cannot be believed by any reasonable person without one. Mere reason is insufficient to convince us of its veracity: and whoever is moved by *Faith* to assent to it, is conscious of a continued miracle in his own person, which subverts all the principles of his understanding, and gives him a determination to believe what is most contrary to custom and experience.

Yet this kind of wickedly witty scoffing at the Christian complex of belief and faith—this temptation of the Scorner—might rather be seen as a reason for excluding than for including Hume in the context of Coleridge's "willing suspension of disbelief." What allows Hume's phantom hand to reach into the company of Plato, Paul, and Kant to give the phrase its distinctive cross-twist from unbelief to disbelief is a weightier, more complicated, and more equivocal consideration. In the *Treatise of Human Nature,* published in 1739, Hume devotes an extensive analysis to the mental action of belief. Thus in book 1, part 3, chapter 7 is called "Of the nature of the idea, or belief," chapter 8 is "Of the causes of belief," and chapter 10 is "Of the influence of belief." Part 3 itself bears the title "Of knowledge and probability," and in it as well as in preceding sections, discussion is carried on in the specific context of an analysis of the idea of imagination.

Indeed, so germane is all this to the elements of poetic fiction addressed in Coleridge's passage, that Hume at one point notes directly, " 'Tis certain we cannot take pleasure in any discourse, where our judgment gives no assent to those images which are presented to our fancy." He continues:

The conversation of those, who have acquir'd a habit of lying, tho' in affairs of no moment, never gives any satisfaction; and that because those ideas they present to us, not being attended with belief, make no impression upon the mind. Poets themselves, tho' liars by profession, always endeavour to give an air of truth to their fictions. . . .

Following this train of thought, Hume asserts that "poets have form'd what they call a poetic system of things, which tho' it be believ'd neither by themselves nor readers, is commonly esteem'd a sufficient foundation for any fiction. . . ." Hume insists that "belief must please the imagination by means of the force and vivacity which attends it; since every idea, which has force and vivacity, is found to be agreeable to that faculty." Though he says that "the least reflection dissipates the illusions of poetry, and places the objects in their proper light," he amends this conclusion by saying, " 'Tis however certain, that in the warmth of a poetical enthusiasm, a poet has a counterfeit belief, and even a kind of vision of his objects."

Hume's "counterfeit belief" is so close to Coleridge's "mere poetic Analogon of faith" that only the Scottish philosopher's position as apostle of unbelief, one surmises, prevents him from being the most powerful of all those figures exerting torque on Coleridge's passage in chapter 14 of the *Biographia Literaria*. His hand is there, however, because of a concession he makes in his hostile analysis. The succeeding larger section of his treatise, that is, part 4, is entitled "Of the sceptical and other systems of philosophy," and here his Pyrrhonism is most evident, as are his attacks on the ideas of God, the immortality of the soul, and even personal identity. Arguing that "all knowledge degenerates into probability," he interposes, however:

> Shou'd it here be ask'd me, whether I sincerely assent to this argument, which I seem to take such pains to inculcate, and whether I be really one of those sceptics, who hold that all is uncertain, and that our judgment is not in *any* thing possest of *any* measures of truth and falsehood; I shou'd reply, that this question is entirely superfluous, and that neither I, nor any other person was ever sincerely and constantly of that opinion.

There follows, in an extended argument of subtle nuance, a continued double assertion, where Hume devastates all pretensions to knowledge while simultaneously conceding—he places the concession in italics—that "after all we retain a degree of belief, which is

sufficient for our purpose, either in philosophy or in common life."
He maintains that "the sceptic still continues to reason and believe,
even tho' he asserts, that he cannot defend his reason by reason."
More specifically, Hume argues that though we cannot prove the
continued existence of objects when we are not perceiving, "we may
remove the interruption by feigning a continu'd being," and he says
that "we not only *feign* but *believe* this continued existence."

Hume had originally raised the problem of belief as part of his
attack on causality, arguing that "belief of the existence joins no new
ideas to those, which compose the idea of the object" and that "belief super-adds nothing to the idea, but only changes our manner of
conceiving it, and renders it more strong and lively." At the same
time, however, he accepts the word *belief* in its significance in ordinary speech, and this double valuation accounts for the double
weight of his use of the word.

Hume condensed and reargued this equivocal conception of the
role of belief in his *Enquiry into the Human Understanding* of 1748.
The analysis in this later work, further advertised by the reappear-
ance of the *Enquiry* in his *Collected Essays* of 1777, caught the
interest of German intellectuals. Because in German, as in Greek,
a single word renders the force of both *belief* and *faith*, the concession about *belief* took on added overtones. "The Attic philosopher,
Hume," wrote Hamann to Kant in 1759, "needs faith if he is to eat
an egg and drink a glass of water."

With *belief* shading into *faith* in the single word *Glaube*, in 1785
Hamann's close friend Friedrich Jacobi urged in his *Briefe über die
Lehre des Spinoza* that "das Element aller menschlichen Erkenntniss
und Wirksamkeit ist Glaube"—"the fundamental component of all
human knowledge and effectiveness is faith." By 1787 Jacobi, who
was a radical rationalist trying to save the emotional guarantees of
Christianity and the human soul from the ravages of Enlightenment
raison, set forth a full-blown *Glaubensphilosophie* in an important
treatise called *David Hume über den Glauben, oder Idealismus und
Realismus.* One of the interlocutors in this dialogue says that he has
been reading Hume's essays. The other says, "Against faith, therefore?" and the first one replies unexpectedly, "For faith," whereupon
the second interlocutor challenges him to "make me acquainted with

Hume as teacher of faith." Jacobi's volume was one of the first treatises that Coleridge read in Germany in 1798, and he fully appreciated its argument. As he says at one point in marginal notation: "This is not a fair Criticism on Jacobi. What was his Object? To prove that FAITH, which the Philosophers of his Day, held in contempt, was sensuous Evidence. . . . No! But to prove that the sensuous evidence itself was a species of Faith and Revelation."

Thus Hume, so alien to Coleridge's interests in the expressed premises of his unbelief, is purified by his passage through German *Glaube*, in somewhat the same manner, as it were, that illicit money in the United States is laundered by passing it through Mexican banks. With his settled *unbelief* pulled diagonally into the skeptical *disbelief* that must covertly rely on *belief* and thus become a form of *Glaube* or "faith," Hume takes his place beside Plato, Paul, and Kant in the creation of Coleridge's idiosyncratic formula, "the willing suspension of disbelief."

The translational exchanges or equivalent meanings generated by the foregoing consideration of the phrase "the willing suspension of disbelief" make up a reticulated cultural system reaching backward into the past and forward into the future, linking together concerns of poetry, criticism, philosophy, and theology. The entire network, however, though radiating from Coleridge's commitment to the idea of "faith," does not reveal or even participate in the meaning by experience that made him accept the conception as so very important. The equivalent meanings emanate from but in no way transform or convey the transcendent meaning that sets them in motion.

But what, in this cultural expansion, has "the willing suspension of disbelief" become? To vary the metaphor, the phrase is like a grain of sand in the oyster of cultural forms; successive attention by later critics, and the urgent interconnections from Coleridge's own knowledge and tendency, combine to convert it into a larger entity that is different from its matrix and from its bare original formulation. The larger entity, or pearl, if one wishes, no longer relates to a cultural form; it has become instead an autonomous shape of culture. With a few more layerings of cultural interpretation, indeed, it would not seem especially fanciful to visualize a university catalogue offering a full-term course in The Willing Suspension of Disbelief, involving segmented awareness of many cultural forms. But the course would be chatter, too.

A second significance derives from the very act of interpretation. In the world of quantum physics, which the Nobel Prize winner Richard Feynman has recently declared to be fully understood by no one, it seems that the very act of measuring produces certain of the subatomic realities with which physicists are concerned. Such, mutatis mutandis, is one relation of shapes of culture to forms of culture. The best criticism, as Wilde says, "treats the work of art simply as a starting point for a new creation." "I would call criticism a creation within a creation. For just as the great artists, from Homer and Aeschylus, down to Shakespeare and Keats, did not go directly to life for their subject matter, but sought for it in myth, and legend, and ancient tale, so the critic deals with materials that others have, as it were, purified for him, and to which imaginative form and colour have been already added." The lateral search for meanings that produces interpretation or criticism does not simply illuminate; it also creates new cultural reality.

But the cultural forms it quarries, in their existence as forms rather than as laminated segments of a shape of culture, cohere vertically rather than laterally; they are held in place by history and chronological sequence. Their stability, however, is illusory. Though chronological in their own cultural existence, whenever they are mated with meaning their chronological validity is compromised. The efficacy of chronology proves to be mythical, and its undergirders of support for forms of culture are not stainless steel but rusted iron.

So we may now proceed to a concluding chapter for this brief volume of intimations and hints about a momentous topic: the subversion of forms of culture by shapes of culture. Chronological seriality, which holds together that apprehension of the past in which cultural substance consists, cannot stand close examination. Indeed, McTaggart, in *The Nature of Existence,* argues logically that time itself is unreal. "It seems highly paradoxical to assert that time is unreal, and that all statements which involve its reality are erroneous," he says. "Yet in all ages and in all parts of the world the belief in the unreality of time has shown itself to be singularly persistent. . . . In philosophy, time is treated as unreal by Spinoza, by Kant, and by Hegel. . . . I believe that nothing that exists can be temporal, and therefore time is unreal." After logical argument, he concludes: "Nothing is really present, past, or future. Nothing is really earlier or later than anything else or temporally simultaneous with it. Nothing really changes. And nothing is really in time."

To be sure, C. D. Broad, in his *Examination of McTaggart's Philosophy,* subjects his colleague's arguments to lengthy and severe criticism (as have others), with the conclusion that "I believe that McTaggart's main argument against the reality of Time is a philosophical 'howler' of the same kind as the Ontological Argument for the existence of God." But Broad also concedes that "I am well aware how easy it is to talk nonsense about Time, and to mistake for arguments what are in fact merely verbal tangles. I think it is quite possible that I may have done this. I have altered my mind too often on this most perplexing subject to feel any confidence that my present opinions are either correct or well-founded." And Michael Dummett, reexamining McTaggart's proof, concludes "above all that his argument is not the trivial sophism which it at first appears."

Heidegger, again, urges in *Was heisst Denken?* that "it is time, it is high time finally to think through this nature of time," and in due course he says:

> If all metaphysics thinks of being as eternity and independence of time, it means precisely this: the idea of beings sees them as in their being independent of time, the idea of time sees time in the sense of a passing away. What must pass away cannot be the ground of the eternal. To be properly beings in their being means to be independent of time in the sense of a passing away.

But the philosophers are too abstract for our purposes here, which require an examination denser in texture and more explicit in cultural detail than they provide. If we narrow and intensify inspection to a single cultural focus, the hermeneutic limitations of the chronological approach to criticism, we may be able to glimpse the shifting and adventitious alignments of structure and emphasis that really subsist behind the chronological myth.

5

THE
MYTH
OF
CHRONOS

That the activity of interpretation should be involved with time is a truism: the work being interpreted arises in time, and the hermeneutic endeavor also takes place in time. Less truistic, however, are the paradoxes that arise from any closer examination of the temporal matrix, and they are not resolved by repeated publication on the topic. Studies of literary time abound, as do studies of philosophical time. Not only does Poulet not hold the field alone, but the bibliography of time studies is growing exponentially. On the very day I write this paragraph, for instance, I note that Cornell University Press announces a volume by Wolfgang Holdheim called *The Hermeneutic Mode: Essays on Time in Literature and Literary Theory.* Yet it is no exaggeration to say that all such studies partake of Augustine's perplexity: "What then is time? If no one asks me, I know; if I wish to explain it to one that asks, I know not."

The concept of time is insecure both in its befores and afters. It is only by a later conflation that the mythical Kronos is identified with the Greek word for time, for the titan's name is not the same word as the temporal *chronos;* and it is only because the titan's name began to be used to indicate a superannuated dotard, and perhaps also because Old Father Time's scythe seemed compatible with the sickle wielded by Kronos, that the two entities could seem to merge. And far from existing in monolithic permanence, the mythical Kronos was embattled on all fronts. Probably pre-Hellenic in his own lineage, he is threatened by his past—his sickle, we learn, is the implement used to castrate his father Uranus. He is equally embattled with his future, for he himself is overthrown by his son Zeus. The motif of borders being folded into the middle and the middle reappearing at the borders, of the outside becoming inside and the inside outside, is emphasized by Kronos's nasty but effective habit of eating his children. Yet he is then forced to disgorge them by Zeus, who has gone into his maw not as Zeus but only as a stone wrapped in swaddling clothes. Zeus himself, meanwhile, cannot be located by Kronos, either in heaven or on earth or in the sea, for his mother has suspended him in a cradle hanging betwixt all three.

It is in contemplating this kind of paradox—enfolding and regurgitation and elusiveness—that Augustine rises to a pitch of wonder: "I confess to Thee, O Lord, that I yet know not what time is, and again I confess unto Thee, O Lord, that I know that I speak this in time." He wrestles mightily with the paradox:

> I say boldly that I know, that if nothing passed away, time past were not; and if nothing were coming, a time to come were not; and if nothing were, time present were not. Those two times then, past and to come, how are they, seeing now the past is not, and that to come is not yet? But the present, should it always be present, and never pass into time past, verily it should not be time, but eternity. If time present . . . only comes into existence, because it passes into time past, how can we say that either this is, whose cause of being is, that it shall not be so; so, namely, that we cannot truly say that time is, except because it is tending not to be?

He exclaims, "My soul is on fire to know this most intricate enigma." He does see that the past folds into the present:

> Wheresoever then is whatsoever is, it is only as present. Although when past facts are related, these are drawn out of the memory, not the things themselves which are past, but words which, conceived by the images of the things, they, in passing, have through the senses left as traces on the mind. Thus my childhood, which now is not, is in time past, which now is not: but now when I recall its image, and tell of it, I behold it in the present, because it is still in my memory.

The future, too, he sees, folds into the present:

> We generally think before on our future, and that forethinking
> is present, but the action whereof we forethink is not yet, be-
> cause it is to come. . . . Which way soever then this secret fore-
> perceiving of things to come be; that only can be seen, which
> is. But what now is, is not future, but present. . . . I behold the
> daybreak, I foreshow, that the sun is about to rise. What I be-
> hold, is present; what I foresignify, to come; not the sun, which
> already is; but the sun-rising, which is not yet. And yet did
> I not in my mind imagine the sun-rising itself . . . I could
> not foretell it. But neither is that daybreak which I discern in
> the sky, the sun-rising, although it goes before it. . . . Future
> things then are not yet: and if they be not yet, they are not: and
> if they are not, they cannot be seen; yet foretold they may be
> from things present. . . . What now is clear and plain is, that
> neither things to come nor past are. Nor is it properly said,
> "there be three times, past, present, and to come": yet perchance
> it might be properly said, "there be three times; a present of
> things past, a present of things present, and a present of things
> future."

But though Kronos can engorge both past and future into his maw of
the present, the elusive Zeus remains outside, and ultimately the
stone is disgorged along with the ingested children:

> But how is that future diminished or consumed, which as yet is
> not? or how that past increased, which is now no longer, save
> that in the minds which enacts this, there be three things done?
> For it expects, it considers, it remembers. . . . Who therefore
> denies, that things to come are not as yet? and yet, there is in
> the mind an expectation of things to come. And who denies
> past things be now no longer? and yet there is still in the mind a
> memory of things past. And who denies the present time has no
> space, because it passes away in a moment?

For Augustine this shifting and insubstantial complex is approached
by measuring, which itself is of ambivalent efficacy:

> We measure times as they pass. And if any should ask me,
> "How do you know?" I might answer, "I know, that we do mea-

sure, nor can we measure things that are not; and things past and to come, are not." But time present how do we measure, seeing it has no space? It is measured while passing, but when it shall have passed, it is not measured; for there will be nothing to be measured.

If we extrapolate Augustine's probings for the concerns of literary interpretation, we shall see, mutatis mutandis, that his emphasis on measuring is coordinate with the emphasis on chronology with which literary history presents us the writers and texts we interpret. The Augustinian prologue to the hermeneutic uses of chronology, with its testimony to elusiveness, is necessitated by our critical-historical tendency to take chronological considerations as an interpretative absolute. One must insist, on the contrary, that chronological facts are as deeply enmeshed in paradox as is the temporal matrix from which they arise. If the conflation of *chronos* as time with the myth of the titan Kronos is a misprision, such misprision can serve as "representative anecdote" for the inauthenticity of any chronological linearity. As Pausanias confessed, writing in the second century, he used to look upon such stories as that of Kronos and his father "as markedly on the foolish side," but later his opinion changed, and he "guessed that the Greeks who were accounted wise spoke of old in riddles and not straight out, and that this myth about Kronos is a bit of Greek wisdom." Its wisdom is available for us too, and its meaning with reference to the hermeneutic status of chronology is delphically presented in Coleridge's summation, a fortnight before he died, with the entirety of his past life present to his gaze: "I am dying, but without expectation of speedy release. Is it not strange that very recently bygone images, and scenes of early life, have stolen into my mind, like breezes blown from the spice-islands of Youth and Hope—those twin realities of this phantom world."

The world demarcated by chronology is a phantom world too; the world of reality is something quite other. What follows in this discussion will attempt to indicate some of the reasons how and why this is so, and to illustrate as well the limits and inadequacies of chronology as an interpretational instrument, whether we attempt to apply it to cultural sequences, to the events in a creating consciousness, or to a work itself.

With regard to the hermeneutics of an individual work, any text we wish to interpret is, in the manner of Keats's Grecian urn, approached as timeless. It is presented to us as a total present, that is, as an object of intuition. The process of interpretation may then historically locate it within a time scheme, but at the outset it stands outside such coordinates. In its inner being as statement it may, like Yeats's "Sailing to Byzantium," be riddled by temporal reference, but as an object for interpretation it engages our attention outside time, and it is the same text whether we attempt to analyze it on Wednesday or decide to wait until Thursday. This engagement of attention, however, is in the nature of a false present, or at least a hypothetical present, for the work has been produced in a past.

In like manner, other time indications are not what they seem. We refer to the production of the work in the past not as a property of that past but as a process in the creating consciousness of an author. That is to say, the work has had to be composed within a sequence that we denature by thinking of it as psychological rather than temporal, though in fact it is ineluctably temporal. The work may, furthermore, come before or after other works by the same author, and in that case we generally relate it to its position in such a sequence. Though a moment's reflection shows that a work is what it is even if anonymous, and must, as New Critical theory emphasized, be taken on its own terms as an object without historical, psychological, intentional, or other external reference, already the paradoxes of the chronological approach emerge by the fact that we nevertheless always relate individual works to their author's existence and to his or her other works. There is no judge of paintings for whom it does not make a difference that *The Night Watch* is by Rembrandt. Derek Traversi has argued, indeed, that the proper approach to a Shakespearean play—it is an approach in any event universally utilized as unstated ground-rule of Shakespearean commentary—is to see the play in its role in the entire sequence of Shakespeare's plays: "Among the most fruitful aspects of recent Shakespearean criticism," writes Traversi "has been the realization that there exists, behind the long and varied sequence of the plays, a continuous development of theme and treatment which makes it impossible to regard any of them, even the greatest, as mere isolated masterpieces." This statement occurs in a book called *Shakespeare: The Last Phase,* and one need only briefly reflect on the pregnancy of that title as an indication of the hermeneutic approach to the dramatist's meaning. Certainly when Maurice Morgann considered *The Tempest* to be a revision of an earlier version of the play that "in its original state was Shakespeare's *first* dramatic work," the play could not be interpreted as containing the final wisdom that we all now ascribe to it, and Morgann's commentary to *The Tempest* accordingly indicates no such wisdom.

Leaving aside, at least for the moment, the chronological relation of a given work to other works by the same author, we may take up the fact noted earlier, that the individual work has a chronological sequence in its inner development. Not until a work is finished do we begin to interpret it, but its state of being finished is a chronological terminus in the author's effort. When Coleridge presents "Kubla Khan" as an unfinished fragment, he is clearly attempting to deflect criticism, even though we may think the poem is about as finished as any poem in our language; but we do note the efficacy of declarations of completion or incompletion for the certainties of criticism. The basis for interpretation and for future editions is thus, to use a phrase from Bowers's *Principles of Bibliographical Description,* "the latest corrected state of the text." But even here paradox intrudes, for Bowers, in his *Textual and Literary Criticism,* gives choice illustrations of why such a text might not be the best, concluding that "the latest author-revised edition of a modern writer, is, I should say, often less trustworthy than a scholarly edition of an older author." The point has recently been documented a fortiori by Gabler's monumental reedition of Joyce's *Ulysses,* which thoroughly subverts the published version as authoritative text.

Jonathan Wordsworth mounts an even more radical challenge to the chronological identification of the work as the author's last effort. In *The Music of Humanity: A Critical Study of Wordsworth's Ruined Cottage,* he produces a text of Wordsworth's poem in accordance with a principle that the best version of an author is not the last but the first, before its freshness has been dissipated by revision. "On the whole," he says,

> poets are known by the best versions of their works: Wordsworth is almost exclusively known by the worst. De Selincourt, of course, published the 1805 version of *The Prelude* as early as 1926, but the bulk of Wordsworth's work is still read in reprints of the last edition of his lifetime. Most poems lose by this, but none loses more than the *Ruined Cottage*. As Coleridge remarked, "Poetry, like schoolboys, by too frequent and severe correction may be cowed into dullness." Written in 1797–8, *The Ruined Cottage* was revised again and again before being published as Book I of *The Excursion* in 1814; and extremely important changes were made in the text which is most commonly read as late as 1845.

Jonathan Wordsworth reiterates this position in his *William Wordsworth: The Borders of Vision*, where he endeavors—he says that "it is clearly important"—to quote Wordsworth's poetry "in its earliest surviving versions." In 1941 Raymond Dexter Havens said, "By '*The Prelude*' is generally understood *The Prelude* of 1850. It has always been so; presumably it always will be so." Jonathan Wordsworth, however, not only prefers the 1805 version—along with Herbert Lindenberger, Stephen Gill, and others—but in a paper called "Seventeen Versions of the Prelude" he makes it clear that of all versions he regards the 1850 as the worst. Indeed, in collaboration with M. H. Abrams and Gill he has recently presented an edition containing not only, as has been customary in recent years, the thirteen-book 1805 version along with the fourteen-book 1850 version, but also the embryonic 1799 version in two books. His followers even hint that this embryonic version might be the best of all.

Yet, despite these assaults on the chronological terminus, Jonathan Wordsworth, in massive paradox, does not reject the importance of chronological considerations. Quite the contrary, he elevates them to supreme and substantive importance. He regards himself ultimately as being precisely a chronologist, and in *William Wordsworth: The Borders of Vision*, he says:

Some may feel that I emphasize too frequently the dates and facts of composition, but the circumstances in which the poetry was written altered very much during Wordsworth's most creative years, and only a sharp sense of chronology can enable one to isolate qualities of mind and art that stay the same. . . . With an awareness of chronology one can see literary structure as counterpointed against the patterns of composition.

He carries over this emphasis into his practice as a reviewer; of one important work, he makes what he regards as a weighty charge by saying that it "fudges" chronology. By this he means not that it cites mistaken dates, which we perhaps agree would be poor scholarship, but rather that it does not accord portentous significance to minutely demarcated befores and afters.

But that "fudging chronology" should be an important consideration to that reviewer directs attention to the role and nature of chronology and allows us to illuminate the insubstantiality, or at least the limitations, of chronology as a hermeneutic instrument. Chronology, we must insist, has no interpretational substance, only an interpretational function. Its truth is schematic, not inherent. What do we mean by saying that chronology and its interpretive use are not inherent but schematic? Two things. First, that chronology does not pertain to the actual experience of time; secondly, that its use by an interpreter is merely an *Auslegung*, a mode of arranging data. It arises from his or her taxonomic commitment, not from the data themselves.

As to the first point, that chronology does not pertain to the actual experience of time, a brief consultation with one's own experience should serve to validate the point. For instance, I sometimes feel called upon to revise pages in my own work, sometimes more than once. I often indicate these later revisions by a mark such as "second version," "third version," or at other times I simply put a date at the top of the revised page. If the first draft bears the notation May 18 and the second May 22, I know that the later date indicates the revised version. But I sometimes neglect to put any mark whatever at the top of the page, and as a result I have more than once been embarrassed, when looking through draft pages, to find that I cannot tell which is the original version and which the revised version, although the corrections or changes seemed clamorously demanded at the time I made them. The point is that only a radical improvement would indicate inherently which was the later version. A chronological marking would indicate the sequence, to be sure, but without that marking the sequence could not be established except by the inherent difference of quality in the two versions.

To take this insistence from the personally empirical to the public and theoretical, one might avail oneself of the arguments of Bergson, in his *Essai sur les données immédiates de la conscience*. Bergson points out that homogeneous time, which is an abstraction, is not the same as duration, which is the actual experience of time, or time proper. Duration, however, is purely qualitative, not quantitative. As Bergson suggests, "pure duration might well be nothing but a succession of qualitative changes, which melt into and permeate one another, without precise outlines, without any tendency to externalize themselves in relation to one another, without any affiliation to number." The only way time can be measured, or chronologized, is by "the trespassing of the idea of space upon the field of pure consciousness." Strictly speaking, therefore, duration lies outside chronology, while chronology pertains only to "time, conceived under the form of a homogeneous medium," which Bergson finds "a spurious concept." "At any rate," he continues, "we cannot finally admit two forms of the homogeneous, time and space, without first seeking whether one of them cannot be reduced to the other." Bergson's argument, proceeding from the awareness that "the idea of space is the fundamental datum," thus leads him to conclude that "time, conceived under the form of an unbounded and homogeneous medium, is nothing but the ghost of space haunting the reflective consciousness."

The interpretive analyst, however, needs a unitive pattern on which to arrange his or her heterogeneous data, and one of the most immediately convenient is the framework supplied by chronology. Many organizational problems are solved by this appeal, which like the Fahrenheit scale for measuring degrees of heat and cold, does not inhere in the data but does have a wide recognition factor in the populace. That recognition factor, however, is merely a conventionalized response. We know what it is to be cold, and we can say that it is colder now than it was an hour ago; a novelist may objectify the sense of cold by talking of frosty breath, or the thin sheet of ice on a pool, or the keen and cutting wind. When the novelist says that the temperature is twenty-five degrees Fahrenheit, however, he or she is making a purely schematic statement, not an inherent statement. The specification carries its meaning only by equivalence, not by experience. For instance, when Tolstoy, in *War and Peace*, speaks of "the calm frost of twenty degrees Réaumur," the sense of cold is conveyed only by the word *frost*, not by "twenty degrees Réaumur"; we do not recognize the Réaumur scale, and so it is only when a note by the translator informs us that twenty degrees Réaumur is "13 degrees below zero, Fahrenheit," that we can correlate this more familiar convention with our sense of cold.

In like manner, Marx's title *The Eighteenth Brumaire of Louis Bonaparte* uses a date from the new calendar set up by the French Revolution; few of us remember now, however, what month Brumaire was supposed to be. We may remember that the eighteenth Brumaire was the date on which Napoleon the First came to power in France, and we may have a further memory that converts this information to the chronological schematism 1799, but without a reference we still probably cannot convert it to a specific month. Furthermore, Napoleon did come to power at a lived moment in time, but this moment existed only for those in proximity to him, not for an Eskimo in Northern Canada.

Without procedural safeguards, however, one tends to take the chronological arrangement to have meaning in itself. Not only does it not possess such meaning, but to ascribe such meaning to it distorts our true understanding of the contours of experience. We seem to be saying something just and true when we note that Wordsworth was born in 1770, that he published *Lyrical Ballads* in 1798, that he married in 1802, that he died in 1850. On April 23, 1850, however, when he died, Wordsworth might have been aware that it was spring and that he was dying; he certainly had no awareness of all those days since 1802. Perhaps, like Coleridge, he had intimations of youth and hope, those twin realities of this phantom world.

What an individual remembers and what a chronology asserts are not identical, and indeed, the difference is the stuff of misinterpretation. A single example can be supplied from Coleridge. His first volume of poetry, entitled *Poems on Various Subjects,* was published on 16 April 1796. But when he published his *Biographia Literaria* in 1817, he said in retrospect that "in 1794, when I had barely passed the verge of manhood, I published a small volume of juvenile poems." The scholar Norman Fruman has noted the discrepancy as an example of Coleridge's untruthfulness; on the contrary, one must insist that it is simply a testimony to the difference between memory and chronology. Lest one think that twenty-one years cannot jostle the conventional alignment of memory and chronology, let one simply recall some occasion when one has kept a diary, neglected a week's entries (indeed, sometimes merely a day's), and then tried to straighten out the events for chronological recording. Proust's great novel, which is one of literature's most monumental testaments to the mining of past experience, repeatedly distinguishes the different contours of duration from that of chronologically homogeneous time, as Mann also does in presenting the experience of Hans Castorp in his mountain sanatorium.

Both Proust and Mann wrote before Bakhtin formulated his theoretical elucidations of novelistic time-representation. What Bakhtin's analyses everywhere indicate is the literary disintegration of conventional lines of chronology. Such lines are displaced and rewoven into elements of place and value, and sometimes negated entirely. As Bakhtin says in his discussion of the Greek romances, which were the earliest "novels": "all of the action in a Greek romance, all the events and adventures that fill it, constitute time-sequences that are neither historical, quotidian, biographical, nor even biological and maturational. . . . In this kind of time, nothing changes: the world remains as it was. . . . This empty time leaves no traces anywhere, no indications of its passing."

The analysis of "adventure-time" in the Greek romance ("for Greek adventure-time to work, one must have an *abstract* expanse of space") is a specific observation of what Bakhtin calls a "chronotope"—"the intrinsic connectedness of temporal and spatial relationships that are artistically expressed in literature." Of chronotopicity in literature as a whole (there are differing chronotopes, such as "the meeting," "the castle," "the threshold") he concludes:

> A literary work's artistic unity in relationship to an actual reality is defined by its chronotope. Therefore the chronotope in a work always contains within it an evaluating aspect that can be isolated from the whole artistic chronotope only in abstract analysis. In literature and art itself, temporal and spatial determinations are inseparable from one another, and always colored by emotions and values.

But even if one concedes these points with reference to "novelistic" time, biography or autobiography—the actual record of a human life—would seem bound to chronology and in need of its supports. Even here, however, we find the chronological *Auslegung* to be of equivocal import. To be sure, we remember our own birthdays, and we want to know when our biographical subject was born, flourished, and died; but this knowledge pertains not to chronology but to the human process of waxing and waning—"birth, copulation, and death"—and to the relational structure of the intellectual or political community in which the subject functions. In fact, the more rigorously a biography begins at the beginning and proceeds by chronological steps to the end, the less vital it tends to be; one may even hazard that this constitutes a universal truth: the more responsibly precise the observation of chronological markings, the duller the resulting text.

The reason is not far to seek. Chronological markings impose a Procrustean evenness upon the varying contours of actual experience. Such evenness, however, is always more the conventionalized response of cultural conditioning than a reflection of reality. As Stephen Greenblatt notes, in his *Renaissance Self-Fashioning:*

> So fully do we inhabit this construction of reality that most often we see beyond it only in accounts of cultures immensely distant from our own: "The Nuer [writes Evans-Pritchard] have no expression equivalent to 'time' in our language, and they cannot, therefore, as we can, speak of time as though it were

something actual, which passes, can be wasted, can be saved, and so forth. I do not think that they ever experience the same feeling of fighting against time or of having to co-ordinate activities with an abstract passage of time because their points of reference are mainly the activities themselves, which are generally of a leisurely character. . . . Nuer are fortunate." Of course, such a conception of time and activity had vanished from Europe long before the sixteenth century. . . . Puritans in the late sixteenth century were already campaigning vigorously against the medieval doctrine of the unevenness of time, a doctrine that had survived largely intact in the Elizabethan church calendar. They sought, in effect, to desacramentalize time, to discredit and sweep away the dense web of saints' days, "dismal days," seasonal taboos, mystic observances, and folk festivals that gave time a distinct, irregular shape; in its place, they urged a simple, flat routine of six days work and a sabbath rest.

Yet the autobiographical test with regard to chronological distortion is so important that it requires extended discussion. Take Wordsworth's *Prelude*, for example, an autobiographical venture that is without question the greatest poem of the nineteenth century. Although Wordsworth roughly follows a progression from childhood, through boyhood, Cambridge education, travel on the Continent, and sojourn in France during the French Revolution, there is very little that can be called strictly chronological in his memories. He proceeds by fits and starts, and the sequence is interrupted by such things as book 5, which is called "Books," and book 8, which is entitled "Retrospect: Love of Nature Leading to Love of Man." He admits that "I see by glimpses now," and this testimony to evanescence is confirmed when he goes on to say that his hope is to give "Substance and life to what I feel, enshrining / Such is my hope, the spirit of the Past / For future restoration." The concern here is not for temporal schematism but for "what I feel" and for the "spirit of the Past," not its chronology.

Accordingly, the most characteristic emphasis of his great act of self-recollection is the "spots of time" that he denominates in the twelfth book of the 1850 version. Although he there gives a few special examples of what he means by the phrase "spots of time," in fact he has from the first pressed forward by the repeated invocation of spots of time. Indeed, it is significant that the spots-of-time passage, which occurs in the twelfth book in the latest version of his poem, occurs in the first book of the earliest version, that of 1798–99. Thus the skating scene to which I referred in the second chapter above is ineluctably a spot of time. Such memories are the substance of what Wordsworth feels. And the very nature of spots of time is to be timeless; they are units of experience free from chronological sequence. Wordsworth wrote many of them early—such as the ascent-of-Snowdon passage that eventually came to rest in book 14 of *The Prelude*—and moved them around in his poem in terms of an emphasis of feeling, not an emphasis of chronology. Wordsworth uses his temporal schematism of progression from childhood to adulthood merely as a wire upon which to string his timeless globules of recollection, for the spots of time are both atemporal and unchronological.

Indeed, *The Prelude* cannot proceed at all until he has located the first of these globules. The beginning of the poem is remarkable— Beethovenian, as I have elsewhere said—in its reaching for themes and prospects after it is already under way. Wordsworth, appearing at the start as an adult with all his abilities about him, wants to write a great poem, but he has no topic. He runs through a lengthy list of possible topics, to no avail. By this time he is more than 250 lines into the poem and understandably begins to feel depressed:

> Far better never to have heard the name
> Of zeal and just ambition, than to live
> Thus baffled by a mind that every hour
> Turns recreant to her task; takes heart again,
> Then feels immediately some hollow thought
> Hang like an interdict upon her hopes.
> This is my lot; for either still I find
> Some imperfection in the chosen theme,
> Or see of absolute accomplishment
> Much wanting, so much wanting, in myself,
> That I recoil and droop, and seek repose

> In listlessness from vain perplexity,
> Unprofitably traveling toward the grave,
> Like a false steward who hath much received
> And renders nothing back.

There follows an agonized question about his origins, as he looks into his earliest childhood memories:

> Was it for this
> That one, the fairest of all rivers, loved
> To blend his murmurs with my nurse's song,
>
> .   .   .   .
>
> For this, didst thou,
> O Derwent! winding among grassy holms
> Where I was looking on, a babe in arms
> Make ceaseless music that composed my thoughts? . . .

For Wordsworth to look into his past, however, is for Antaeus to touch the earth; invigorated by invocation of his childhood river, he suddenly discovers in that matrix his first spot of time, his first globule of significant memory:

> Oh, many a time have I, a five years' child,
> In a small mill-race severed from his stream,
> Made one long bathing of a summer's day;
> Basked in the sun, and plunged and basked again
> Alternate, all a summer's day, or scoured
> The sandy fields, leaping through flowery groves
> Of yellow ragwort; or when rock and hill,
> The woods, and distant Skiddaw's lofty height,
> Were bronzed with deepest radiance, stood alone
> Beneath the sky, as if I had been born
> On Indian plains, and from my mother's hut
> Had run abroad in wantonness, to sport
> A naked savage, in the thunder shower.

With this discovery his great theme is revealed to him, and he promptly begins on his gigantic alternation of systolic and diastolic modes, or better still the breathings in and out of his being: first, apostrophe or universal statement, then globule of experience, then apostrophe again or universal statement, then globule of experience. The first apostrophe is the wondrous

> Fair seed-time had my soul, and I grew up
> Fostered alike by beauty and by fear:
> Much favoured in my birthplace. . . .

The first globule following this apostrophe is the memory of stealing game from other hunters' snares. The second apostrophe or universal statement is

> Dust as we are, the immortal spirit grows
> Like harmony in music. . . .

The second globule is the boat-stealing episode. The third apostrophe is "Wisdom and Spirit of the universe," after which two more globules of recollection are beaded onto his attempt to trace his being's earthly progress, the first a memory of "November days . . . When, by the margin of the trembling lake / Beneath the gloomy hills I homeward went / In solitude," and the second the immortal skating scene. The fourth apostrophe, "Ye Presences of Nature in the sky / And on the earth!" is followed by two more globules. None of these intensities is chronologically demarcated; all are representations of the spirit of the past, not of its measurement. Indeed, the very globule that sets it all in motion, "Oh, many a time have I, a five years' child," is quite willing to bend chronology, for certain differences exist between the globule and the lines that are offered in the 1799 version, which reads as follows:

> Beloved Derwent, fairest of all streams,
> Was it for this that I, a four years' child,
> A naked boy, among the silent pools
> Made one long bathing of a summer's day,
> Basked in the sun, or plunged into thy streams,
> Alternate, all a summer's day, or coursed
> Over the sandy fields, and dashed the flowers
> Of yellow grunsel; or, when crag and hill,
> The woods, and distant Skiddaw's lofty height,

> Were bronzed with a deep radiance, stood alone,
> A naked savage in the thunder-shower?

It is significant that Wordsworth does not change the attempt to get at the essence of experience; in both the 1799 and 1850 versions the line "Made one long bathing of a summer's day" is the same, as is "Basked in the sun" and "all a summer's day"; but just as among other changes "yellow grunsel" is changed to "yellow ragwort," so does "four years' child" become "five years' child." Chronology is here merely a rhetorical option of the surface, not the essence of the experience.

If we consider another great effort of self-recollection, one that in some sense might be called the Bloomean strong precursor of Wordsworth's, we will realize that Rousseau's *Confessions,* though seemingly more overtly chronological than Wordsworth's remembrances, is really hardly more precise. It, too, uses chronology merely as a wire to bead together complexes of memory. True, Rousseau informs us that he was born in 1712, and the *Confessions* continues to 1765, specifically schematized in chronological segments. Thus book 1 in little bursts spans the years 1719–23 and then 1723–28, book 2 1728–31, book 3 1728–31 and 1731–32, book 4 1731–32 and 1732, book 5 1732–38 and then 1737–41, book 6 1737–41, and so forth through book 12, which ends in 1765. Not only does the irregularity of the chronological confrontation compromise temporal demarcation at the outset, but on the very first page Rousseau warns us that "if by chance I have used some material embellishment it has been only to fill a void due to a defect of memory. I may have taken for fact what was no more than probability, but I have never put down as true what I knew to be false."

Such an indication of another kind of ebb and flow underneath the chronological surface occurs again and again. "My first part has been entirely written from memory, and I must have made many mistakes in it," Rousseau calmly says at the beginning of book 7. "Being compelled to write the second from memory also, I shall now probably make still more." Yet again, he stresses that

> I am writing entirely from memory, without notes or materials
> to recall things to my mind. There are some events in my life

that are as vivid as if they had just occurred. But there are gaps and blanks that I cannot fill except by means of a narrative as muddled as the memory I preserve of the events. I may therefore have made mistakes at times, and I may still make some over trifles, till I come to the days when I have more certain information concerning myself. But over anything that is really relevant to the subject, I am certain of being exact and faithful, as I shall always endeavor to be in everything.

What was really relevant to the subject, for Rousseau as for Wordsworth, was the sense of the gathering of being that the gaze into the past brought with it. As Rousseau says of that time he calls "the short period of my life's happiness":

. . . how can I tell what was neither said, nor done, nor even thought, but only relished and felt, when I cannot adduce any other cause for my happiness but just this feeling? I rose with the sun, and I was happy; I went for walks, and I was happy . . . I strolled through the woods and over the hills, I wandered in the valleys, I read, I lazed, I worked in the garden, I picked the fruit, I helped in the household, and happiness followed me everywhere; it lay in no definable object, it was entirely within me; it would not leave me for a single moment.

Nothing that happened to me during that delightful time, nothing that I did, said, or thought all the while it lasted, has slipped from my memory. The times preceding it and following it recur to me at intervals; I recall them irregularly and confusedly; but I recall that time in its entirety, as if it existed still. My imagination, which in my youth always looked forward but now looks back, compensates me with these sweet memories for the hope I have lost for ever. I no longer see anything in the future to attract me; only a return into the past can please me. . . .

Rousseau's testament to the "sweet memories" that compensate for the "hope I have lost for ever" and that stand out clearly against other parts of his past, which can be recalled only irregularly and confusedly, are a version of Coleridge's "youth and hope," the twin realities of this phantom world.

In truth, except that Wordsworth's *Prelude*—his "poem to Coleridge" as he usually called it—is written in lofty poetry and reflects the elevated attitudes of Wordsworth's egotistical sublime, and that Rousseau's *Confessions* is written in prose and reflects the self-humiliating abnegations of Rousseau's masochistic personality, the two testaments are remarkably similar. Hazlitt acutely observed of Rousseau:

> The only quality which he possessed in an eminent degree, which alone raised him above ordinary men, and which gave to his writing and opinions an influence greater, perhaps, than has been exerted by any individual in modern times, was extreme sensibility, or an acute and even morbid feeling of all that related to his own impressions, to the objects and events of his life. He had the most intense consciousness of his own existence. . . . His ideas differed from those of other men only in their force and intensity. His genius was the effect of his temperament. He created nothing, he demonstrated nothing, by a pure effort of the understanding. His fictitious characters are modifications of his own being, reflections and shadows of himself. . . . Hence his excessive egotism, which filled all objects with himself, and would have occupied the universe with his smallest interest.

From this consideration of Rousseau's self-preoccupation, Hazlitt—presciently, in view of the fact that he did not know *The Prelude*—proceeds to compare Rousseau with Wordsworth:

> Rousseau, in all his writings, never once lost sight of himself. . . . He owed all his power to sentiment. The writer who most nearly resembles him in our own times is the author of the *Lyrical Ballads*. We see no other difference between them, than that the one wrote in prose and the other in poetry. . . . Both create an interest out of nothing, or rather out of their own feelings; both weave numberless recollections into one sentiment, both wind their own being round whatever object occurs to them.

A closer examination would reveal both the similarities and idiosyncratic differences of the two autobiographers. Take as single example the odd fact that both Wordsworth and Rousseau present among their earliest significant recollections not one but two episodes of boyhood theft. In book I of Wordsworth's *Prelude* we learn of the theft of other people's snares, with a characteristic admonitory moral animism in the memory:

> Sometimes it befell
> In these night wanderings, that strong desire
> O'erpowered my better reason, and the bird
> Which was the captive of another's toil
> Became my prey; and when the deed was done
> I heard among the solitary hills
> Low breathings coming after me, and sounds
> Of undistinguishable motion, steps
> Almost as silent as the turf they trod.

Alongside this we may place Rousseau's first, characteristically nearridiculous, memory of theft in his own book I:

> There was a journeyman at my master's by the name of Verrat, whose mother lived in the neighborhood and had a garden a considerable distance from her house, where she grew very fine asparagus. Now it occurred to M. Verrat, who had not much money, to steal some of her asparagus. . . . As he was not very nimble and did not want to take the risk himself, he picked on me for the exploit. . . . I have never been able to resist flattery, and gave in. Every morning I went and cut the finest asparagus. . . . This little business went on for several days without my so much as thinking of robbing the robber. . . . Thus I learnt that stealing was not so terrible as I had thought; and I soon turned my new knowledge to such good account that nothing I coveted and that was in my reach was safe from me.

Wordsworth's second memory of theft, the boat-stealing episode, is even more pregnant with moral animism than the first:

> One summer evening . . . I found
> A little boat tied to a willow tree
>
> .   .   .   .
>
> Straight I unloosed her chain, and stepping in

Pushed from the shore. It was an act of stealth
And troubled pleasure. . . .

. . . .

She was an elfin pinnace; lustily
I dipped my oars into the silent lake,
And, as I rose upon the stroke, my boat
Went heaving through the water like a swan;
When, from behind that craggy steep till then
The horizon's bound, a huge peak, black and huge,
As if with voluntary power instinct
Upreared its head. I struck and struck again,
And growing still in stature the grim shape
Towered up between me and the stars, and still,
For so it seemed, with purpose of its own
And measured motion like a living thing,
Strode after me. With trembling oars I turned,
And through the silent water stole my way
Back to the covert of the willow tree;
There in her morning-place I left my bark,—
And through the meadows homeward went, in grave
And serious mood; but after I had seen
That spectacle, for many days, my brain
Worked with a dim and undetermined sense
Of unknown modes of being; o'er my thoughts
There hung a darkness. . . .

As Wordsworth's second episode continues the grave tone of the first,
so Rousseau's continues his own near-burlesque chatter:

One memory of an apple-hunt that cost me dear still makes me
shudder and laugh at the same time. These apples were at the
bottom of a cupboard which was lit from the kitchen through a
high lattice. One day when I was alone in the house I climbed
up on the kneading trough to peer into this garden of the Hes-
perides at those precious fruits I could not touch. Then I went
to fetch the spit. . . . I probed several times in vain, but at last I
felt with delight that I was bringing up an apple.

He is unable to get the apple out, however, so:

Next day, when the opportunity offered, I made a fresh attempt. . . . But unfortunately the dragon was not asleep; the larder door suddenly opened; my master came out. . . . Soon I had received so many beatings that I grew less sensitive to them; in the end they seemed to me a sort of retribution for my thefts, which authorized me to go on stealing. . . . I reckoned that to be beaten like a rogue justified my being one.

Despite their wide difference in tone, the recollections by both autobiographers have a common form as globules of experience. They are episodes symbolic of larger meanings, not tributes to chronological accuracy. Thus, despite their difference in moral stance, they both by their nature as theft testify to their authors' notable tendency, remarked by Hazlitt, to ingest all reality into their own selfhoods, while on the other hand they are located very imprecisely in time. Rousseau, in fact, in that same first book confesses that "I know nothing of myself till I was five or six. I do not know when I learned to read."

This same contour obtains with respect to Rousseau's great confessional predecessor Augustine (who also records a stealing episode, that of some pears, early in his recollections). If we look at Augustine's *Confessions,* indeed, we see even less chronological substance than we do in Rousseau. We find in Augustine only sporadic concern with precise chronology, which is subordinated to his attempt to gather the meaning of a life together as witness to the grace of God. At the end of book 1, in fact, he specifically identifies chronological segments as being merely representations of a mysterious larger unity: "Yet, Lord, to Thee, the Creator and Governor of the universe, most excellent and most good, thanks were due to Thee our God, even hadst Thou destined for me boyhood only. For even then I was, I lived, and felt; and had an implanted providence over my well-being—a trace of that mysterious unity whence I was derived. . . ."

As the example of Augustine's *Confessions* lay behind those of Rousseau, Rousseau's own influence streamed into another great autobiographical venture, the *Mémoires d'outre-tombe* of his romantic successor Chateaubriand. Here too we find chronology merely a schematism, and an imperfect one, for the essence of memory. Indeed, the fluctuations by which inside becomes outside and outside inside, by which things of the center become those of the periphery and those of the periphery supplant those of the center— fluctuations that characterized the state of Kronos in his myth—are transliterated by Chateaubriand's own "Testamentary Preface" to his masterpiece:

> The *Mémoires,* divided into books and chapters, have been written at different times and in different places: these divisions naturally give rise to kinds of prologue that recall the incidents that have occurred since the last dates, and depict the places where I pick up the thread of my story. The varied events and the changing forms of my life thus enter into one another; at moments of personal prosperity I may talk of times when I was poor, and in days of tribulation I may recall days of happiness. The various feelings of my various times of life, my youth encroaching on my old age, the gravity of my years of maturity saddening my green years; the rays of my sun, from its rising to its setting, crossing and merging like the separate reflections of my existence, impart a sort of indefinable unity to my work: my cradle has something of my grave about it, my grave something of my cradle, my suffering becomes pleasure, my pleasure pain, and one cannot tell whether these *Mémoires* are the work of a young head or of an old head.

Notable in this testament is Chateaubriand's identification of time not in terms of linear demarcations but in terms of the ebb and flow of life: youth, old age, years of maturity, green years, the cradle, the grave, and above all "times of life," not its chronological scale.

If chronological considerations are equivocal even in autobiographical ventures, where one would expect to find them most efficacious, in other forms of culture they have scarcely any purchase at all and indeed lead to serious distortion. The rubric of Traversi cited above, *Shakespeare: The Last Phase,* symbolizes the paradoxical involvement of individual works in a sequence of authorial composition; but titles such as George Sherburn's *The Early Career of Alexander Pope* or Émile Legouis's *La Jeunesse de William Wordsworth* symbolize another truth whose roots go even deeper.

For the early career, or the youth, of a cultural figure could never become the subject of elucidation until the whole of the career and the whole of the life were already lived. Dilthey supplies a theoretical formulation of this experienced truth in his tract called *Die Entstehung der Hermeneutik*, where he emphasizes that "the chronological succession" of various works or thoughts "is of less moment" than the apprehension of a "systematically constructed whole."

What are the considerations that guarantee the validity of such a contention? We may isolate at least four that interlock in their effect, ranging from the practical and locally specific through the psychoanalytic, the organic, and finally the hermeneutically formal. As to the first, an example might be a modern commentator's remark about Coleridge:

> It is difficult to work out a satisfactory chronology for the development of Coleridge's metaphysics, partly because so much of the evidence is in manuscript form and still awaits editing, and partly because Coleridge himself appears to advance by fits and starts, circling round and round, recalling fragments of discarded theory and jettisoning thoughts more recently adopted.

Complementary to this remark by J. R. de J. Jackson is the observation by Richard Ellmann that developmental chronology is impeded by Freudian *Nachträglichkeit,* the sporadic emergence of timeless unconscious materials into the temporal concerns of an author.

Ellmann's observation can serve as a bridge to the second, or psychoanalytic, consideration that works against the reality of chronological demarcations of development; for in psychoanalytical awareness our lives are the unfoldings of a drama whose roles were cast and whose plot was sketched at the beginning of our existence. As Mircea Eliade has noted, in his volume called *Myths, Dreams and Mysteries:*

> One of Freud's discoveries above all has had portentous consequences, namely, that for man there is a "primordial" epoch in which all is decided—the very earliest childhood—and that the course of this is exemplary for the rest of life . . . whatever the adult's attitude may be towards these primordial circumstances

they are none the less constitutive of his being . . . *the essen-*
tial human condition precedes the actual human condition

Eliade's conclusion runs radically counter to ordinary assumption,
and if it is true it follows that the markings of chronological division
can never be of essential importance.

Thirdly, the archaic reality signalized by Eliade's dictum, re-
defined by psychoanalysis, is parallel to and intertwined with such
doctrines as that of Platonic anamnesis and Aristotelian entelechy,
both of which pertain to the conception of organic form. All underlie the striking declaration of Leibniz quoted at the end of the first
chapter above, that

> it is a bad habit we have of thinking as if our psyches received
> certain forms as messengers and as if it had doors and win-
> dows. We have all these forms in our minds, and even from all
> time, because the mind always expresses all its future thought
> and already thinks confusedly of everything of which it will
> ever think distinctly. Nothing can be taught us the idea of which
> is not already in our minds. . . . This Plato has excellently rec-
> ognized when he puts forward his doctrine of reminiscence.

Leibniz was the great early annunciator of the Romantic doctrine
of organic form, and this quotation, which underlies that doctrine,
might almost be the epigraph for this whole book.

The doctrine of organic form, based on the reciprocity of bloom
and seed, leads directly into the historical theory of hermeneutics. It
is customary to divide historical hermeneutics along a watershed
from Schleiermacher to Dilthey in the nineteenth and early twentieth
centuries and from Heidegger to Gadamer in our own era. All statements of that theory, however, are explicitly linked together, and
they all derive from the intense interaction of seminal figures in German Romanticism—Friedrich Schlegel, Schelling, and Schleiermacher. Though Schleiermacher propounded hermeneutic doctrine
most influentially, it seems as though Schlegel might actually have
been slightly prior in the redefining of the Leibnizian heritage. As
Dilthey notes, "Friedrich Schlegel became Schleiermacher's mentor
in philology. The concepts developed by the former in his brilliant

essays on Greek poetry, Goethe and Boccaccio, were those of the inner form of a work, of the evolution of a given writer as a systematic whole."

But such an evolution by its very nature renders substantively irrelevant the demarcations of chronology. As Wordsworth trenchantly asks:

> who shall parcel out
> His intellect by geometric rules,
> Split like a province into round and square?
> Who knows the individual hour in which
> His habits were first sown, even as a seed?
> Who that shall point as with a wand and say
> "This portion of the river of my mind
> Came from yon fountain?"

Wordsworth's reference to the seamlessness of river and fountain rebukes the surface divisions of chronological schematism, as does his invocation of the idea of organic form under the aegis of the word *seed*. In fact, Wordsworth's very word, *seed*, was central for Schleiermacher. As the commentator Rudolf Makkreel says:

> Schleiermacher's heuristic method of explicating and clarifying the intentions of an author had appealed to a doctrine of a *Keimentschluss* (seminal decision of an author). This organic image of a seed (*Keim*) from which a work grows, not only serves as a suggestive clue for interpreting the unity of a work, but is also used as a psychological core idea to *explain* the overall character of the work.

Again, Schleiermacher's pupil, the classical philologist August Boeckh, places organic form squarely at the base of hermeneutic presupposition:

> A literary work is, as Plato noted (*Phaedrus* 264C), an organism; but in an organism the whole precedes the parts. The artist in fact holds the whole of this work, undeveloped, before his

spiritual eyes, as a unified perception, from which all its parts are developed as limbs of the whole. In this unity of the work is concentrated the individuality of the author, and it must thus be grasped by means of individual interpretation and pursued in its further organization.

What Boeckh here emphasizes lies at the very heart of formal hermeneutics. Dilthey, for instance, in speaking of Schleiermacher's *Methodenlehre,* says that "we always know the whole only in the part and the part only through the whole." He is propounding a topos not only from Schleiermacher but from high Romanticism as well. Schelling, for instance, says that "there is no true system that is not at the same time an organic whole. . . . If in every organic whole everything supports and underlies everything else, then this organization would have to exist as a whole in pre-existence to its parts; the whole could not arise from the parts, rather the parts would have to arise from the whole." It is evident that this description of organic form works against the dominance of chronological concerns, for if development is the unfolding of something already there, the arbitrary markings of chronology may schematize but not affect its substance. As I have elsewhere said, "Chronology, it is true, can often have a specific value; but its reverence by the scholarly tradition is largely a convention of that tradition, complementing the scholarly prejudices that require 'development' in the sense of progressive steps. The textbooks exult in the proliferation of developmental stages; but such stages do not allow us to see clearly the unfolding of a single, constant orientation to life." In line with this truth, Georg Brandes says at the outset of his intellectual biography of Goethe that there will be no "stages" and no "rubrics." Of all rubrics those supplied by chronological tagging are the most arbitrarily schematic and the most destructive of organic awareness.

Schelling's insistence on the organic priority of the whole to its parts was transferred by his follower, the classical philologist Friedrich Ast, into the definition of the hermeneutic circle (*Zirkel, Kreis der Erklärung*): that we cannot understand a work except through its component parts, while we cannot understand these parts without an original sense of the whole: "Auch hier tritt der oben bemerkte Zirkel ein," he summarizes at one point, "das nehmlich das Einzelne nur durch das Ganze und umgekehrt das Ganze nur durch das Einzelnen verstanden werden kann."

Ast has earlier said, somewhat modifying Schelling's view of the priority of the whole:

> The basic law of all understanding and knowing is to find the spirit of the whole from the part and to grasp the part through the whole. . . . But both are posited only with and through one another, so that the whole cannot be thought without the part, as its member, nor the part without the whole, as the sphere in which it lives. Neither precedes the other, because both simultaneously condition one another and constitute a single harmonious life.

He later argues, however, seeming to rejoin Schelling:

> The circle (*Zirkel*), that I can know a, b, c etc. only through A, but A itself only through a, b, c etc. is insoluble, if both A and a, b, c are thought of as opposites that reciprocally limit and presuppose one another but their unity is not recognized, so that A is not first produced out of a, b, c etc. and formed by them, but produces them itself, penetrates them all in the same manner; a, b, c accordingly are nothing other than individual representations of the One A. . . . Therefore A already lies in each one in a special manner, and I do not first need to run through the whole infinite series of individual parts in order to find their unity. . . . The spirit is never something assembled out of parts, but rather an original, simple, undivided essence. In each part therefore it is just as simple, whole and undivided as it is in itself, that is, each part is only a particular, apparent form of the One Spirit. . . .

Ast was here writing in 1808, in a treatise called *Grundlinien der Grammatik, Hermeneutik und Kritik*. His formulation preceded Schleiermacher's. As Gadamer, for instance, says, "Schleiermacher follows Friedrich Ast and the whole hermeneutical and rhetorical tradition when he regards as an essential ingredient of understanding that the meaning of the part is always discovered only from the context, i.e. ultimately from the whole."

Gadamer goes on to stress that the critical effect of the hermeneutic circle is that "the movement of understanding is constantly from the whole to the part and back to the whole." Chronological understanding, on the contrary, is always linear; it not only cuts through the circle but is an entity of a completely different and ultimately irrelevant order. A straight line is the antithesis of a circle; experience is not linear but globular.

Indeed, we may formulate a concluding dictum: any interpretational or critical act that takes chronological linearity as pertaining to the reality of things must be factitious in its conclusions. As a single example of such factitiousness we may take a special version of the chronological fallacy, this one urged by Stanley Fish. Fish argues, in his *Surprised by Sin: The Reader in Paradise Lost*—and the contention is important for his conception of the reader's edification—that "the reading experience takes place in time, that is, we necessarily read one word after another," and that "the childish habit of moving the eyes along a page and back again is never really abandoned although in maturity the movement is more mental than physical." "The questions we ask of our reading experience," he accordingly says, "are in large part the questions we ask of our day-to-day experience. Where are we, what are the physical components of our surroundings, what time is it?"

But we ask such questions neither of our day-to-day experience nor of our reading experience; the statement is as factitious as the interpretation of Milton it is designed to serve. Against Fish it must be urged that although we read in the direction of a work's forward movement, we interpret the work, as it were, backward. Not until we have grasped a work as a whole can we begin the process of interpretation. Then we look back from this whole and only then conceive the interpretive task. Even so simple an interpretive function as a book review does not begin until the reviewer has finished the book. The reviewer's discursive language of review begins not immediately following his or her discursive apprehension of the work, but only after the discursive apprehension has been replaced by the unitive intuition of the whole book: unless the unitive intuition supervenes, there cannot follow the second discursion.

In other words, no one writes an interpretation of *Hamlet* until he or she knows the whole play. Furthermore, Fish's notion of chronological progression across and down the page really has no relationship to anyone's experience of *Hamlet,* interpreter or not, because the outcome of *Hamlet* is never a secret in our cultural awareness. Can anyone remember when he or she really did not know how the play turns out? In any event, there can be no chronological surprises for the hermeneutic analyst, as there can be none for the student. For the idle reader, possibly; for the critic, never.

Fish in effect thinks of the linear progression of reading as a kind of continuous writing on a tabula rasa of the reader's mind. But that is not the way the interpretive reader proceeds. Coleridge argues that two factors are necessary to any method: first, unity, and secondly, progression. "For Method," he says, "implies a *progressive transition,* and it is the meaning of the word in the original language. The Greek μέθοδος is literally a *way* or *path of Transit.*" But to use this path there must be a signpost, a sense of where the path is going, and this third factor Coleridge calls "pre-conception"; there must always be what he calls a "mental antecedent," or what he also calls a "pre-cogitation *ad intentionem ejus quod quaeritur.*" He explicitly says that these "scientific principles" are a "forcible illustration of the Aristotelian axiom, with respect to all just reasoning, that the whole is of necessity prior to its parts." "Without continuous transition, there can be no Method," he says, but "without a preconception there can be no transition with continuity."

Coleridge's insistence on what he calls "a previous act and conception of the mind" as necessary to all method has had the richest kind of succession in later thought. Michael Polanyi's influential writings in the theory of scientific method have been based on precisely such a principle: scientific experimenters, contrary to what we are taught in our early schooling, do not follow strict laws of induction, to surprise themselves with unforeseen results; rather, they proceed with an intuition of the outcome of their experiments. So, too, hermeneutic theory has taken up the principle of "pre-conception" or "pre-cogitation," which works so direly against Fish's assumptions, into the very heart of its conceivings. Dilthey speaks of the interpreter's "reconstructive understanding": "At first it encompasses the whole in a presentiment (*Ahnung*) until it raises the whole to a conscious unity informed by knowledge of particularity. Herewith the circle implicit in the concept of interpretation is solved insofar as the individual components can only be understood from the whole and vice versa." Alongside Dilthey's "presentiment" we may place Heidegger's conception of the fore-structure of understanding (*Vor-Strucktur des Verstehens*), a fore-structure that ramifies into the hermeneutic triad of anticipation of meaning or fore-having (*Vorhabe*), of seeing in advance (*Vorsicht*), and of a fore-conception in which we grasp something in advance (*Vorgriff*). Coleridge's insistence on the necessity of "pre-conception" or "pre-cogitation" emerges again in the thought of Gadamer, who speaks of "fore-conception": "The circle of understanding . . ." he says, "describes an ontological structural element in understanding. The significance of this circle, which is fundamental to all understanding, has a further hermeneutic consequence which I may call the 'fore-conception of completion.' It states that only what really constitutes a unity of meaning is intelligible." "One's own fore-understanding," he says again, is "the first of all hermeneutic requirements." Such "fore-understanding" takes up again the "forethinking" and "secret fore-perceiving" of Augustine.

These animadversions, directed against the assumptions implicit in Fish's commitment to temporal linearity in the process of understanding, are not adventitious; they pertain rather to the very nature of interpretive activity. In this function they rebuke also Jonathan Wordsworth's merry phrase, "fudging chronology." Mark Reed's *Wordsworth: The Chronology of the Early Years* and its companion volume on the middle years serve as a kind of Bible for the chronological faith of Jonathan Wordsworth; but William Wordsworth himself rejected all manifestations of "that false secondary power / By which we multiply distinctions, then / Deem that our puny boundaries are things / That we perceive, and not that we have made." In his mathematical treatise *The Direction of Time,* Hans Reichenbach, after musing on the relation of past, present, and future, sets up four axioms. Statement 1: "Time goes from the past to the future." Statement 2: "The present, which divides the past from the future, is now." Statement 3: "The past never comes back." And Statement 4: "We cannot change the past, but we can change the future." About 250 pages later, after speaking of the "distinction between the indeterminism of the future and the determinism of the past," which is expressed in the laws of physics, he says that "the concept of *becoming* acquires a meaning in physics: The present, which separates the future from the past, is the moment when that which was undetermined becomes determined, and 'becoming' means the same as 'becoming determined.'" "The time of our experience is the time which manifests itself through a registering instrument."

In these apprehensions we see the work of literature, the sequence of an author's multiple works, the field of culture as such, or any other experiential continuum, as a kind of zipper. The past, or the already determined, is the closed part of the zipper; the present, or the registering of now, is the fastener; and the future, or the undetermined, is the separated portion of the zipper. I use this homely but precise illustrative analogy to make clear that for hermeneutic purposes the direction of our approach to a work is of paramount importance. Reading and interpreting are diametrically opposed; to see the zipper from its open side is entirely different than to see it from the closed side. Fish's chronometrical approach is opposed in its very nature to what interpretive activity does. Reading a work is like closing the zipper, rendering the split parts of its indeterminism into the already read and therefore dead past of the zipped up. Interpretive activity reverses this process, moving the registering of now not from past to future but from future to past, opening the closed zipper into its original multiplicity. In so doing it opens the determined matter of the finished book or poem back into the renewed indeterminacy of vitally problematic awareness. The finished mystery story vanishes into the dead past; the interpreted masterpiece is perennially a kind of open future.

Viewed either from past to future or from future to past, chronology itself has no substance. When we actually live our lives, it is in intensities or dilapidations of the spirit that flood out of or contract within the impositions of temporal division; when we look back, either to criticize or to inspect, the latest event in a chronological scheme is indistinguishable from an earlier one. If I wish to think of the Battle of Fontenoy, I use the marking 1745 to zoom in on the event, which promptly fills the cosmos of my attention. If I then think of the Battle of Agincourt, it has no relationship, either as earlier or later, to Fontenoy; the convention, 1415, serves as a file number for information retrieval, and once retrieved, Agincourt too fills the cosmos of my attention. Both battles—both globules of experience—are either wholly absent or, when recalled, fully present in my thoughts. They have no other existence. Their dates are only their file numbers.

So much for the hermeneutic limitations of the chronological approach to culture. With the foregoing analysis the series of suggestions contained in this volume may fittingly find its conclusion. Experience, underneath the chronological superimposition, is as monadic in its structure as are the shapes of culture that have increasingly replaced the nominal linearities of cultural forms; and the schematisms we use so lazily that we deem them to subsist in the nature of things have actually neither substance, nor meaning, nor light for our lives.

The chaos of the modern cultural situation is unlikely to witness another resurgence of formal determinants, and its anarchy will in all probability prevail against attempted reorganizations either of educational systems or of the cultural canon. In time, the limited capacity of human attention will doubtless make it necessary to dismiss many of the cultural objects, and much of the cultural data, currently available to our consciousness. These rejected structures will be relegated to the memories of computers, from which specialists or other computers will only occasionally summon them. But those that remain as subjects of living thought will almost certainly continue to present themselves as monadic shapes of culture, not as chronologically cumulative and culturally interrelated forms. The collective enterprise will continue to advance or, as the case may be, to devastate the social and material interests of humankind. But shapes, validated by the privacy and certainty of individual experience, rather than forms, proffered by the group and its collective mythology, are now becoming, and henceforth will increasingly be, the true bearers of culture.

INDEX